REDEFINING
OPERATIONAL
EXCELLENCE

REDEFINING OPERATIONAL EXCELLENCE

New Strategies for
Maximizing Performance and Profits
Across the Organization

Andrew Miller

AMACOM AMERICAN MANAGEMENT ASSOCIATION

NEW YORK • ATLANTA • BRUSSELS • CHICAGO • MEXICO CITY
SAN FRANCISCO • SHANGHAI • TOKYO • TORONTO • WASHINGTON, D.C.

Bulk discounts available. For details visit:
www.amacombooks.org/go/specialsales
Or contact special sales:
Phone: 800-250-5308
Email: specialsls@amanet.org
View all the AMACOM titles at: www.amacombooks.org
American Management Association: www.amanet.org

This publication is designed to provide accurate and authoritative information in regard to the subject matter covered. It is sold with the understanding that the publisher is not engaged in rendering legal, accounting, or other professional service. If legal advice or other expert assistance is required, the services of a competent professional person should be sought.

Library of Congress Cataloging-in-Publication Data

Miller, Andrew
  Redefining operational excellence : new strategies for maximizing performance and profits across the organization / Andrew Miller. — First Edition.
    pages cm
  Includes bibliographical references and index.
  ISBN-13: 978-0-8144-3397-3
  ISBN-10: 0-8144-3397-9
  1. Performance. 2. Organizational effectiveness. 3. Management—Technological innovations. I. Title.
  HF5549.5.P35M5495 2014
  658.4'012—dc23
                                                    2013048835

About AMA

American Management Association (www.amanet.org) is a world leader in talent development, advancing the skills of individuals to drive business success. Our mission is to support the goals of individuals and organizations through a complete range of products and services, including classroom and virtual seminars, webcasts, webinars, podcasts, conferences, corporate and government solutions, business books, and research. AMA's approach to improving performance combines experiential learning—learning through doing—with opportunities for ongoing professional growth at every step of one's career journey.

Printing number

10 9 8 7 6 5 4 3 2 1

CONTENTS

Chapter 6:

ACQUIRING AND KEEPING THE CUSTOMERS YOU WANT

Chapter 7:

OPTIMIZING SPEED MAXIMIZES PROFITABILITY

Chapter 8:

CENTERS OF EXCELLENCE: NOT SO MUCH

ACKNOWLEDGMENTS

THIS BOOK WOULD NOT HAVE BEEN POSSIBLE without some very special and supportive people.

I want to thank my agent, Jeff Herman for believing in my ideas so strongly that he agreed to represent me on the same day that he was introduced to me.

To my publisher AMACOM, and specifically senior acquisitions editor Bob Nirkind, it has been a pleasure working with you and I thank you for seeing the same need as I did for a book like this. You have been supportive throughout this process and provided useful insights and suggestions along the way.

To Dr. Alan Weiss, thank you for convincing me to submit the original book proposal, for guiding me along the way, and for introducing me to Jeff Herman. This would never have happened without your subtle and not-so-subtle pushes.

To my colleagues—Colleen Francis, Amanda Setili, Stuart Cross, Linda Henman, Kim Wilkerson, Chad Barr, Seth Kahan, Roberta Matuson, Bill Lee, and Richard Martin—thank you for providing your insights and your experience to help make the process of writing this book a pleasure.

A sincere thank you to my wife, Eryn, and my children, James, Nicki, and Ellie for supporting me throughout this process. I truly appreciate your ongoing love and affection.

To my parents, and my family and friends, thank you for all of the support and positive reinforcement.

To all of the excellent companies out there, thank you for giving me a reason to write this book and providing me with great examples to use.

INTRODUCTION

OPERATIONAL EXCELLENCE IS THE RELENTLESS PURSUIT of doing things better. It is not a destination or a methodology but a mind-set that needs to exist across an organization. Operational excellence is not about perfection or performing activities. It is about providing dramatic performance improvements and financial growth.

In my more than 15 years of consulting with some of the world's best-known organizations, I have seen firsthand how some of these organizations rely on methodologies like Lean and Six Sigma as they try to work toward operational excellence. I have also seen how such methodologies reliably fail to deliver sustainable results. Operational excellence is about empowering employees to use judgment on the front lines, but often an organization uses methodologies that preclude having to use judgment. The methodology becomes a crutch.

That was why I needed to write *Redefining Operational Excellence*. After seeing so many organizations succeed briefly and then fail, and others never succeed at all, I wanted to show how organizations can pursue operational excellence in a new way—one that sheds reliance on methodologies and tools and that focuses instead on good judgment in the best interest of the organization and its customers.

To achieve dramatic results, you must create a different culture for your organization—a culture that questions current operating models and focuses on adding value and optimizing speed. *Redefining Operational Excellence* will help you define and implement that culture.

It will show you how a culture of operational excellence helps increase profitability, effectiveness, retention of personnel and customers, engagement, empowerment, innovation, performance, and many other positive effects. It will help you achieve money and performance boosts in areas where organizations don't normally look. And it will enable you to determine the optimal speed at which your organization can operate by implementing indicators that measure progress and success, not just activity completion.

We will look at what the most successful companies in the world do to reach heights and achieve results they once thought impossible. Do you ever wonder why companies like Disney, Apple, 3M, BMW, and General Electric continue to achieve tremendous success while others flounder? It's because they operate better than anyone else does; they find opportunities to increase profitability and performance where no one else looks.

Redefining Operational Excellence brings together strategies for enacting the four components of operation excellence—attracting and retaining top talent, innovating and collaborating, aligning strategy and tactics, and acquiring and keeping the customers you want—and provides insights into the value of optimizing the speed (when to act quickly, when to slow down) at which your organization operates.

Chapter 1 tackles old ways of thinking. It looks at the way most organizations approach operational excellence and why that approach is flawed. I discuss the limitations of various methodologies and set the stage for why we need a new way to approach operational excellence.

Chapter 2 then opens the discussion of the four core components and explains how to create an organization that focuses on them.

Chapters 3–6 examine each of the four components more deeply, offering practical strategies and numerous tips to help you understand and implement the ideas presented in these chapters quickly and effectively.

Chapter 7 does the same for the idea of optimizing the speed at which your organization operates.

Chapter 8 looks at the concept of a center of excellence and why it makes no sense. If an organization can't be excellent in all areas, why would it think it could be excellent in one? I focus on the reasons excellence doesn't stick and provide commonsense approaches to success.

Chapter 9 focuses on five specific industries: retail, services, health care, technology, and manufacturing. For each, I offer examples of companies that are performing well and insights about why.

Chapter 10 explores how technology supports operational excellence, with examples of organizations that are effectively using technology to improve results and performance.

Chapter 11 considers the future of operational excellence and what organizations can do now to ensure their continued success. The way we measure success needs to change, and I show how organizations can not only achieve tremendous success but also sustain it. I will show you how to raise the bar for your organization so that you can stay ahead of the competition.

The Appendix offers a short assessment tool that will help you identify the level of excellence in your organization. In addition, there's a link to a more comprehensive diagnostic you can use to identify areas of your organization that provide the best opportunities for improved performance and profitability.

Operational excellence happens on the front lines of your organization when employees are empowered to make decisions and use their judgment. It doesn't require a certification or a degree or a colored belt, but it does require drive and a commitment to the pursuit of excellence.

Redefining Operational Excellence has something for every business, large or small. The organizations that will derive the most from it are the ones who have the ability and the desire to change the way they operate in order to dramatically improve their financial and organizational performance.

Welcome to the new world of operational excellence. I hope you plan to stay a while.

CHAPTER 1

THE NEED FOR
A NEW DEFINITION

ORGANIZATIONS HAVE USED THE TERM *operational excellence* for years, although there is no common understanding of what it really means. Is it a methodology or a mind-set? Is it focused on processes or results? Where do customers and employees fit in? Until recently, operational excellence has generally been associated with manufacturing and production, but that is changing.

The old connotation of operational excellence—focused on manufacturing throughput, standardizing processes, and eliminating waste—is a relic. It's time has passed. Our world is too complex, too interconnected, and too fast moving to focus solely on solving problems and standardizing processes. Today's customers are well educated, and today's employees need to be more empowered in order to stay engaged.

The old associations that organizations made with operational excellence have grown stale; our thinking about operational excellence has changed. Companies now recognize the value of improving performance not only on their production lines but also in the ways their employees interact with customers, suppliers, and other business partners.

Operational excellence is a journey, not a destination. This more holistic view of a company and what it does changes the way organizations do business. This chapter and ultimately this book will outline why that change is necessary and how to go about making it.

THE BEGINNINGS OF OPERATIONAL EXCELLENCE

The current association we have with operational excellence derives from our experiences with such methodologies as Six Sigma and Lean manufacturing.

Six Sigma focuses on the elimination of all flaws in a process and the standardization of processes wherever possible. It encourages companies to strive for perfection in any process.

In the 1980s, Motorola developed Six Sigma as a way to use data and statistics to remove defects from their manufacturing processes. It has since been adopted by many other organizations, most notably by Jack Welch and General Electric (GE) in the 1990s. Organizations took the initial concept and applied it outside manufacturing to other business processes, with varying results.

Lean focuses on the elimination of waste within a specific process or activity. It was developed, also in the 1980s, for the Toyota Production System as a way to eliminate waste in manufacturing processes. Toyota's principles focused on removing waste from the process in order to maximize customer value. As with Six Sigma, Lean has been adopted in general business processes to help companies focus on creating value for the customer.

Both Six Sigma and Lean have their benefits, but they also have their limitations.

The Limitations of Six Sigma

The assumption is that companies employing Six Sigma automatically achieve operational excellence, but the truth could not be more different. Making use of Six Sigma as the equivalent of operational excellence is like saying, "I have a black belt in karate; therefore, I am a martial arts expert." Six Sigma is only a small component of operational excellence, one of many methodologies employed to achieve it.

Six Sigma focuses on the removal of the root cause of errors (defined as elements that fail to meet customer expectations) and on minimizing variability in processes. Essentially, Six Sigma helps you fix root problems and maximize standardization, but those two efforts alone do not result in operational excellence.

When asked to identify companies we consider operationally superior, Dell, Amazon, Apple, Disney, and Walmart come to mind. Are these companies operationally excellent because they fix root problems and maximize standardization, or is their operational excellence due to their quality management system? The answer is neither. They are operationally excellent because they go well beyond these activities. These companies engage their customers, they constantly innovate, they continuously improve how they operate, and they move at optimal speed. They may use Six Sigma approaches, but applying Six Sigma does not equal operational excellence.

Six Sigma principles never would have helped Apple develop the iPod or motivated Dell to develop an approach for customers to customize their own computers through the Internet. Six Sigma never would have helped Disney develop a customer-first culture where employees are expected to drop everything they're doing to replace a child's ice cream that fell on the ground.

Those innovative ideas didn't start with a problem that needed resolution. They came from a different way of thinking, a different mind-set that was focused on people and customer loyalty and effecting change.

Why Lean Makes You Fat

Today, we try to "lean" everything. We have lean approaches in health care, banking, pharmaceuticals, and many other industries.

The limitation with Lean is that it focuses on the removal of waste and the preservation of value, but not on the actual *creation* of value. Lean might help restore previous levels of success, but it doesn't help you achieve greater heights. Lean is too often used as a methodology, not as a mind-set. Organizations focus on tools and methods, not on changes and behaviors. People are trained in the lean methodology but not so much in the lean mind-set.

When you focus on tools and methods, you become a slave to them and tend to deemphasize, if not remove altogether, critical thinking about growth and value creation.

Lean is an effective way to increase productivity for repeatable tasks, but it doesn't help develop new ideas or strategies.

Don't rely on methodologies and tools as crutches to avoid using judgment. Instead, focus on critical thinking and common sense.

Operational excellence comes from the ability to relentlessly pursue improvements in performance and profitability by focusing on value for the customer. Unfortunately, Lean provides a much narrower focus than that.

REDEFINING OPERATIONAL EXCELLENCE

Methodologies have their place and can be effective as management tries to improve performance in a specific area of an organization or attempts to resolve issues. But methodologies are limited in their ability to drive operational excellence and consider holistic strategies. For true operational excellence, we need a more comprehensive approach that is focused on people and on effecting change.

Companies need to engage the voices of customers and business partners to drive innovation, execution, continuous performance improvement, and, ultimately, profitability. Again, operational excellence needs to happen on the front lines of your organization; it happens when employees are empowered to use judgment that is in the best interest of the organization. When methodologies are used, they are often relied on so heavily that employees don't have to use judgment. When you take away the ability of employees to use their judgment, they quickly lose interest, become less engaged, and default to the tools. This is not a recipe for success.

Figure 1-1 depicts the components of operational excellence for an organization:

- Attracting and retaining top talent
- Innovating and collaborating
- Aligning strategy and tactics
- Acquiring and keeping the customers you want

The figure also depicts that each of these components is enhanced by the ability to optimize speed and is motivated by the impulse to maximize profitability (or, for not-for-profit organizations, effectiveness). Chapter 2 expands on each of these components, and, starting with Chapter 3, I devote one chapter to each. Chapter 7 highlights the important role optimizing speed plays in the effective operation of the four components.

How many of these components do methodologies like Six Sigma and Lean relate to? Very few. So how can we use them

Figure 1-1. The Components of Operational Excellence

synonymously with the term *operational excellence*? We can't. Doing so would be like entering a martial arts competition in which you need to know four different disciplines in order to compete, but you know only karate. You will be great in one area but insufficient in the others.

Operational excellence is the constant pursuit of improved performance and profitability in all areas of your organization. It is about managing talent, driving innovation, aligning strategy and tactics, and enhancing customer engagement. It is about determining optimal enterprise velocity and finding performance opportunities in areas where you don't normally look. Operational excellence is a mind-set, not a tool. It helps increase profitability, productivity, retention, engagement, empowerment, innovation, and many other drivers of an organization.

In a faster, more interconnected world, organizations can't expect to use the same strategies that they have in the past and continue to be successful. Customers, businesses, supply chains, and the skills required to thrive are all changing.

Operational excellence is the constant pursuit of improved performance and profitability in all areas of your organization. It's a mind-set, not a methodology.

Your organization and its approach need to change as well.

When was the last time you looked at your entire supply chain and modernized it? When was the last time you looked at your hiring process? Or your customer acquisition and retention strategies?

If you are like most organizations I deal with, you have probably made incremental changes over the years: purchasing new systems, implementing new processes, and leveraging new management fads. But at the same time, you're still using older processes and technologies. This kind of patchwork process is full of gaps—kind of like a Hershey Air Delight chocolate bar (or an Aero chocolate bar for those who frequent Canada and the UK). It looks solid from the outside but has hundreds of little holes on the inside, and those gaps are having a negative impact on your organization's profitability and other key indicators of success and performance. The sad part is that many organizations don't even know those gaps exist.

Think about your organization as a train. Using patchwork processes to support new products and services is like designing a new, state-of-the-art train and putting it on an old set of tracks. Regardless of how well the new train is built, the old set of tracks will never be able to support the speed and overall maximum performance the new train is capable of. There will always be limitations. There may be delays, maintenance issues, power surges, maybe even crashes.

Organizations need to look at themselves and ask: Are we running a new train on an old set of tracks? The essence of a redefined operational excellence is that it integrates processes and people and strategy and innovation. My new definition of operational excellence can get you that new set of tracks.

Redefining operational excellence means looking at your organization in a different way. We need to take a more holistic view of organizations and the business models they follow. When the overall strategy changes, the tactics the organization employs need to align with that strategy. If you want to attract more global customers, you need to cultivate a more global workforce. If you want to speed up lead times, you need to develop a supply chain infrastructure that can provide consistent support.

WOULD YOU KNOW OPERATIONAL EXCELLENCE IF YOU TRIPPED OVER IT?

Let's get past the theory and pontifications. You want to know what operational excellence smells like and tastes like so that you can pursue it. Because operational excellence is a mind-set, you can set your own goals for success. The final destination (your goals) can and should change again and again because you want to constantly improve how you operate.

Here are some common characteristics of organizations that consistently perform well:

- Their employees are empowered (and empower themselves) to make decisions that are in the best interest of the customer.
- Their products and/or services are of high quality and consistently enhanced, or newer and better ones are routinely developed.
- They perform only activities that add value, and they can measure the role that every activity plays in contributing to that value.

- They have an action-oriented culture.

- They have a clear vision of the future state, and everyone in the organization knows their accountabilities in getting there.

- They are flexible enough to react quickly to market shifts or new market opportunities.

- They have strong relationships with customers and business partners, who act as brand ambassadors and challenge the organization to improve.

- They tie mission to strategy, strategy to execution, and execution to operations.

- They have open and dynamic internal and external collaboration and communication.

- They consistently monitor performance and results.

- They know when to speed things up and when to slow things down in order to maximize results.

- They are able to attract and retain the best people.

If your organization exhibits most of these characteristics, then operational excellence is something that is ingrained in your culture. That doesn't mean that there aren't improvements to be made, but you know that already.

There is no arbitrary end to operational excellence. You need to set your own objectives for success, and those objectives will change over time.

ORGANIZATIONS THAT EXEMPLIFY OPERATIONAL EXCELLENCE

Let's look at three organizations—3M, Disney, and Walmart—and I'll show you how I've scored them and explain why I consider them to be avatars of operational excellence.

(It's important for organizations to know their strengths and to build on those strengths. For details on my more advanced ranking system, please contact me at andrew@acmconsulting.ca; use the subject line "operational excellence ranking system.")

Let's start with Figure 1-2, which shows how I ranked each company (using a scale of one–five, with five being the top score) in each of the main areas of operational excellence.

None of the three companies received a score of five for all of the four components—attracting and retaining top talent, innovating and collaborating, aligning strategy and tactics, and acquiring and keeping the customers you want—and only one got the top score for optimizing speed. It is virtually impossible to perform at the highest level in all five areas. But that doesn't mean that 3M, Disney, and Walmart aren't great examples. (And see my comments later in this chapter about excellence, not perfection.)

3M

3M's strength has always been innovation. It's a company that operates in many different product and service areas and has successfully implemented a culture of innovation. It measures the contribution that new innovations make to its bottom line and challenges its employees to generate new ideas that will be commercially viable. 3M appears to have a mantra stating that a certain portion of their revenue each year should come from products and services that didn't exist five years ago. That shows a strong alignment between strategy (it is a leading company in the area of innovation) and tactics (it has the ability to measure how new innovations impact company performance).

Disney

Disney provides a unique customer experience to everyone who enters one of its properties. Guests are made to feel they have

Figure 1-2. Determining Operational Excellence

	3M	Disney	Walmart
Attracting and retaining top talent	3	4	3
Innovating and collaborating	5	3	4
Aligning strategy and tactics	5	5	5
Acquiring and keeping the customers you want	3	5	4
Optimizing speed	3	3	5

entered a magical fantasy world where they can have anything their heart desires. Here are some ways Disney creates that unique experience:

- Each employee is called a "cast member," making everyone a part of the fantasy world experience that is created when guests enter its properties.
- Every cast member is empowered to make decisions in the best interest of the customer. That might mean handing out a sticker to a child or refilling a spilled drink. The Disney Company is on the front lines and doesn't appear to be hindered by bureaucracy.
- The Disney experience provides something for everyone. Many adults come to Disney without children.
- Disney keeps customers entertained. Even when they are standing in line, they are entertained, so they don't feel they are tediously waiting or wasting time.

◆ The company creates an emotional bond with the customer at every turn. Multiple times per day, customers experience something they have never experienced before (a pop-up parade, a fast pass to a popular ride, early openings and late closings of theme parks), and they will share these experiences with family, friends, and colleagues.

Disney also does a great job of aligning strategy (to provide a great experience for every guest) and tactics (empowering employees to enhance that experience). The company is constantly innovating and making improvements. It engages with customers in various ways and creates unique experiences. It hires the best people, trains them vigorously, and treats them well so that they want to stay with the company.

Walmart

Walmart has always had a very transparent strategy—to offer the lowest prices—and it has always operated in a way that is entirely focused on achieving that strategy. The company has been great at controlling its cost structure and ensuring that customers get the lowest prices possible due to tactics like optimizing its supply chain, sourcing from lower-cost geographies, and working with suppliers to make changes that reduce the cost of production.

Here are some key reasons Walmart exemplifies operational excellence:

◆ It maintains strong collaboration with suppliers and business partners. It will even send in a team of its own employees to work with suppliers to improve the supplier's processes and reduce costs (with an expectation that those cost savings will be passed on to Walmart and, ultimately, to the customer).

♦ The company is always looking for new and innovative ways to operate and for the newest products to offer. It is never satisfied with the status quo.

♦ It engages its customers in the process of selecting new products.

♦ Walmart takes industry leadership positions. For example, it is one of the leaders in implementing sustainability and environmental initiatives.

Figure 1-2 reveals a common theme across all three companies: their ability to align strategy and tactics. (We'll examine this component in depth in Chapter 5.) Even though none of these organizations scored a perfect five in all categories, the fact that they all scored a five in their ability to align strategy and tactics, and they all scored a five in an additional category, makes them good examples of companies to be emulated. Again, companies achieve operational excellence not by striving for perfection but by striving for excellence.

What the Numbers Say

Don't just take my word for the fact that these companies are operationally excellent. Let's look at some of their key financial indicators over the last few years:

♦ Since 2008, the Dow Jones indicator has increased by almost 20 percent. In that same time period, 3M's stock price has increased by more than 40 percent, Disney's by more than 80 percent, and Walmart's by more than 30 percent.

♦ Since 2008, 3M's net income has gone from 13.6 percent to 14.8 percent, representing almost a billion dollars of additional profit.

◆ Since 2008, Walmart has maintained a consistent gross profit margin of nearly 25 percent.

◆ Since 2008, Disney's net income has gone from 12.5 percent to 14.6 percent, representing an additional $1.4 billion in profitability.

These companies improved in key financial areas at a time when the rest of the economy was struggling. The pursuit of operational excellence can indeed yield dramatic results.

WHY OPERATIONAL EXCELLENCE IS IMPORTANT TO ANY ORGANIZATION

Every organization wants to achieve dramatic results, but mission statements or company values don't get results. Developing a great strategy doesn't always lead to great results either, nor does hiring the best people.

An organization needs to strive for excellence in everything it does. It needs to hire and retain the best people. It needs to take great ideas and turn them into commercial products and services. It needs to know when to speed up and when to slow down. It needs to know how to retain and grow with its best customers and acquire new customers.

In pursuing a broad strategy for operational excellence, an organization will consistently gain incremental advantages and improvements that result in maximized performance and profitability. But perfection? That's another story.

Striving for Excellence, Not Perfection

I recently opened a discussion on operational excellence with a LinkedIn group with the statement that organizations need to pursue excellence, not perfection. The other group members thought this was a ridiculous idea. They quoted famous people to prove me wrong and even offered statistics showing why striving for perfection was the right approach.

My response was simple: When you strive for perfection, your only result can be success or failure. If planned performance improvements depend on the organization's achieving perfection, the organization by definition sets itself up for failure. If the planned improvements come in below the level of perfection you are trying to achieve, then the improvements made along the way are not going to be sustainable. Frustration with not being perfect will take over, and the organization will go back to the way it previously operated.

The television has been around for more than 80 years, but it would never have been released if its inventors had tried to make it perfect the first time around. They released a product that was new and worked well, and they continued to make enhancements over time.

Who is able even to determine what perfection is? There are no absolutes in business, so organizations need to identify their own goals for success.

We have this obsession with perfection that actually is a detriment to our success. When we strive for perfection, we make everything black and white. We either achieve perfection or we fail. It's as simple as that.

When you strive for perfection, you can get only one of two results: success or failure. When you strive for excellence, you achieve ongoing improvements that never stop.

But when we strive for excellence, there is no finish line. Excellence is in the eye of the beholder. Each organization and individual has a unique definition of what excellence means.

We never actually achieve perfection. It is an ideal, something that is always just a bit out of reach. The success is in the journey and in the results achieved along the way. An organization may decide to pursue excellence in different areas at different times. It can't be expected to pursue excellence in all areas at once.

Striving for excellence and pursuing it without insisting on perfection allows for incremental improvements. This ability does not exist when we focus on perfection. Typically when organizations try to achieve perfection, they make incremental improvements; however, they fail to take full advantage of them because they are pushing so hard in pursuit of the perfect solution. And until they reach that (unreachable) ideal, they consider their efforts a failure.

There are many examples of software companies that fell in love with making their system perfect for their customers. They held focus groups, delayed launch dates, and constantly made changes. Meanwhile, their competitors launched so-called inferior systems and snatched up all the customers.

When we strive for excellence—however we define it—we remove the pressure to be perfect. We don't have to find the ultimate solution, just one that improves the current situation. Those constant incremental improvements are what separate great companies and great people from everyone else.

We are happy with incremental improvements because we are not chasing an abstract concept of perfection; we are following our own definition of excellence. And we have incremental improvement as a constant goal.

What's your definition of excellence for you and your organization? Once you answer that question, you will have a clearer vision of where you want to be.

REDEFINING HOW WE OPERATE

In this book, I present ways to redefine operational excellence in the most key areas of organizations: their people, their innovation and collaboration, the strategy and tactics, their customers, and the speed at which they operate. It would be difficult for an organization to pursue excellence in all of these areas at once. How will you decide which areas to pursue? Here are five things to consider as you determine where to start in your pursuit of operational excellence:

1. **Benefit.** What are the potential benefits to your organization in pursuing operational excellence in a particular area? Are these benefits financial, nonfinancial, or both?

2. **Risk/Reward.** What is the risk in pursuing operational excellence in a certain area? Might you make things worse? What is the potential upside?

3. **Sustainability.** Can you make sustainable change in this area, or is it going to be only a short-term gain? How can you ensure the sustainability of the right mind-set and the improvements you will make?

4. **Alignment with Strategy and Corporate Strengths.** Are the tactics you want to employ aligned with your corporate strategy? Do you have the ability to implement and execute these tactics successfully? Do these tactics align with your corporate strengths?

5. **Ease of Implementation.** How easy or difficult will it be to make the necessary changes? Is there anything you can do to make the implementation go more smoothly?

There is no one-size-fits-all formula for how to pursue operational excellence. You'll find the answers as you think about where your organization most needs improvement, how to redefine your performance metrics, how to improve your approach to opportunities, and how you will infuse the mind-set of your employees and business partners with a preoccupation with excellence.

Above all, have confidence that a constant focus on incremental improvement is going to improve the way your organization operates.

Chapter 2 goes into more detail about each of the key components of operational excellence and how you can integrate them to get the best results for your organization.

MAKING OPERATIONAL EXCELLENCE HAPPEN

ANY GOOD RECIPE CONTAINS KEY ELEMENTS and ingredients that allow the food to taste great. Operational excellence is no different. Certain elements are required for an organization to become operationally excellent. When those elements are combined properly, a company will see improvements in various areas, depending on their needs, but all companies will see enhanced profitability and growth.

THE CORE COMPONENTS OF OPERATIONAL EXCELLENCE

Figure 1-1 lays out the four key components of operational excellence—attracting and retaining top talent, innovating and collaborating, aligning strategy and tactics, and acquiring and keeping the customers you want—and highlights the importance of optimizing speed toward all four.

This chapter provides a basic definition for each of these components and sets the stage for the in-depth exploration that future chapters will provide.

Operational excellence is the constant pursuit of improving performance and profitability; it focuses on growth and developing new opportunities. Organizations pursuing operational excellence need to ensure that they are looking at success holistically and in all areas of the business.

Many organizations look at themselves as a group of departments that are linked by a common goal and sometimes by common processes. That is the origin of a term like *supply chain*—a chain of events or activities that need to be linked together. But when you look at your organizational functions as being performed by a group of independent, even isolated units held together by a series of links, there will be a lot of opportunities for those links to break or at least weaken.

Organizations must consider every department as a part of the whole. Each department and each function must operate properly in order for the organization to maximize its ability to achieve results. The prevailing attitude needs to be holistic and global, an approach in which excellence makes its way into everything you do: how you hire employees, how you develop and implement strategy, how you generate and commercialize ideas, how you leverage customer relationships, how you resolve customer issues. You need to look at your organization as one organism with a common desired outcome, not as a series of linked departments performing activities.

Figure 2-1 shows the old way of thinking, in which activities and departments are

Your organization should not be a series of linked activities. It is a single organism that must move in unison.

links in a chain that's been built with the goal of getting a product or a service to a customer. The problem is that this way of thinking about an organization means there are gaps between the links, and inevitably some effectiveness and performance is lost in the process.

Figure 2-1. The Old Way: Connecting Links in a Chain

When you have links in a chain, gaps and weaknesses occur. Great organizations are sometimes able to compensate for or even take advantage of those gaps, but a better strategy is to develop a holistic view of your organization and of all the elements that can help make improvements.

Figure 2-2 shows a new way of thinking, in which we are not worried about supporting functions or silos. Instead, we create a common view with a common goal. We bring together everyone involved, both inside and outside the organization, to ensure the success of that common goal and that common purpose.

This new view is what the best organizations are doing right now to differentiate themselves from their competition. They look at the organization as one entity that needs to be aligned in the direction in which it is going and the way it operates. One way of looking at such organizations is that they are resisting the urge to just problem-solve.

Figure 2-2. The New Way: A Holistic Approach

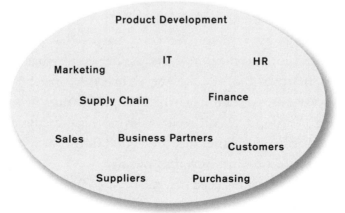

Too often, organizations focus only on problem resolution. When you have an organization made up of links that must be held together and one of the connections weakens or breaks, you need to restore it and strengthen it. This need for repair creates a major limitation on the results that an organization can achieve: The organization can restore itself only to its condition before the break. When you focus on solving problems, you only get yourself back to where you started.

When you focus on operational excellence, you are able to reach new heights and new levels of success through growth and innovation across your organization. My redefinition of operational excellence involves four necessary components for maximum growth and profitability.

Attracting and Retaining Top Talent

"People are the backbone of any organization" seems like a pretty obvious statement. With the exception of some distribution centers that are fully automated, most organizations couldn't run without people.

But if people are so important to every organization, why are so many organizations poor at attracting and retaining the right people? We all know that employees are a key ingredient to the success or failure of any organization, yet we still don't hire well. Why not?

The main reason is that management often doesn't take a bigger view of the organization—where it is going and the skills its people need to get it there. We don't assess what is needed for the organization to achieve its goals and decide whether people are in the right roles and/or have the right skills. Instead, we take the easy way out. For example, when people are not successful, we move them around to different roles within the organization instead of verifying whether they are a good fit for the organization and for the direction in which it's heading.

When organizations need new talent, they focus on activities to be completed, a candidate's experience, and what school she attended. What they should be focusing on is how people deal with certain situations and scenarios, what people in a particular role should be accountable for in terms of results, and what skills people have that are transferable when the industry changes or the organization wants to move in a different direction. In short, focus on what is expected of employees and whether they have the capability to meet or exceed those expectations.

When my clients tell me they are concerned about retaining their best people, I immediately turn the discussion to their hiring process because the best retention strategy begins at hiring. If you are attracting the right type of people to your organization and have an effective process to hire them, then the likelihood of their staying with and contributing to your organization significantly increases. Chapter 3 goes into detail about specific hiring and retention strategies that you can quickly implement to ensure that you are attracting, hiring, and retaining the best people for your organization.

Innovating and Collaborating

Innovation can be disruptive and game changing, or it can be an incremental improvement to an existing product, service, or even process. Innovation means that an improvement was made. Without innovation, an organization stops growing, and when it stops growing, it moves closer and closer to dying. Innovation is the engine that keeps your organization moving in a forward direction; it is paramount to your success that you keep that engine fine-tuned.

Mastering innovation means not only being able to develop good ideas but also encouraging ideas from many different sources, being able to prioritize those ideas, and, most important, being able to turn those ideas into commercial successes. Chapter 4 discusses the cycle of innovation—not only how to generate great ideas but also how to act on them quickly and increase the adoption of the innovation and profitability. It discusses strategies for leveraging employees, customers, suppliers, and other business partners to help identify innovative ideas, as well as how to prioritize those ideas to ensure that you work on only the best ideas. It also discusses the importance of implementing the right metrics as you drive innovation.

The key to innovation is collaboration, which separates the companies that are market leaders from those that are chasing them. Collaboration seems to be a lost art. Organizations get so wrapped up in their daily issues that they forget the value of collaborating with business partners. How often do you meet with key suppliers to align strategies and look for mutually beneficial opportunities? When was the last time you met face to face with key customers? That is where all the action happens, yet many organizations ignore these opportunities.

Aligning Strategy and Tactics

Strategy is the *what*, and tactics are the *how*. As we saw in the examples of 3M, Walmart, and Disney in Chapter 1, the alignment of the *what* and the *how* is generally very high when an organization is successful.

Everyone within an organization needs to understand and support the organization's future vision (its strategy); all employees need to understand what is expected of them (the tactics) as they work to achieve that vision. Day-by-day tactics must align with an organization's desired outcomes. That means aligning not only the tactics but also the metrics for success with that future vision. How people are measured will often determine how they behave.

Chapter 5 discusses in detail the importance of aligning strategy and tactics. It looks at how to align your organization and examines the impact of a misaligned organization. Bringing people together to focus on one common goal sounds easy, but in fact it is very difficult. We need to understand the barriers to having that alignment and develop strategies to remove them.

In the best organizations, everyone lives and breathes the future vision, and everyone knows his or her role in helping to achieve it.

Acquiring and Keeping the Customers You Want

Every organization engages customers in a different way, some more effectively than others. Whatever your strategy, it is important to involve your customers in the operation of your organization. That may mean inviting them to sit on a customer panel, providing them sneak previews of new products, or inviting them to exclusive events. We need to create an emotional bond with our customers and provide them with unique experiences. The best organizations are able to create that emotional bond long before someone becomes a customer.

Chapter 6 discusses how to better engage with your customers and how to leverage their exponential value. It provides strategies to retain your best customers and even strategies on how and when to "fire" customers. I know that is a scary concept, but it is a necessary part of the journey toward operational excellence. Finally, you need to focus on ways to reduce the time and cost of new customer acquisition, and the best way to do that is through your existing customers.

The Importance of Optimizing Speed

Optimizing speed is a concept that few organizations focus on, mainly because no one is talking about the impact it can have on an organization. Chapter 7 discusses the importance of speed within your organization and how to optimize the speed at which your organization acts as you execute the four elements of operational excellence.

Speed optimization means knowing when to speed things up and when to slow things down to achieve better results. The key to doing this successfully is having indicators along the way to guide you.

Every organization knows the importance of speed, but most focus only on moving faster. My clients focus on moving at an optimal speed so that they can achieve better performance and profitability.

EVOLVING TOWARD OPERATIONAL EXCELLENCE

Now let's look at how the key components of operational excellence work together to improve performance.

Operational excellence is a journey with no final destination except great results. But like any great journey, there are landmarks along the way as we get closer and closer to improving how we operate. Organizations need to go through a metamorphosis and transform themselves so that they pursue operational excellence in all areas.

The Five Keys to Mastering the Art of Operational Excellence

An organization that has achieved mastery has implemented a culture of operational excellence and pursues that excellence in everything it does. The goal for any organization is not only to achieve mastery but to sustain it.

Think of the components of mastery as pieces of a puzzle. If one piece is missing, then the puzzle is not complete. To achieve and sustain operational excellence, an organization needs to master these five elements:

Speed. To move quickly through the four phases to mastery, organizations need to learn to optimize the speed at which they act. That means implementing key measurements and indicators to know when to slow down and when to speed up to achieve the best results. (Optimizing speed is covered in detail in Chapter 7.) Many organizations overlook the importance of optimizing speed, to their detriment.

Effective Communication. Successful organizations are very clear about the direction they want to go and are able to succinctly articulate that to employees, customers, business partners, and other stakeholders. They understand who the key stakeholder groups are, what messages need to be delivered to each, how that message will be most effectively delivered, and how frequently to communicate.

Applied Wisdom. Organizations must implement ways to effectively share knowledge internally—across divisions and business units but even within a single department—to ensure that customer case studies and results are shared, communication with customers is streamlined, and key strategic information is conveyed. Often organizations have great internal best practices right under their noses, but they don't do an effective job of sharing them with other departments and business units. Good internal communication—sharing your organization's applied wisdom—is a ready and effective way to improve performance.

Leadership. If you want to move quickly toward mastery, there must be leadership throughout your organization; it can't just be centralized with the executive team. Organizations need to identify key leaders throughout the organization and develop them. There should be opportunities for every employee to step up and take a leadership role, even if it's only for a specific initiative. Often, excellent leaders are found in unexpected areas of the company. Chapter 3 presents an in-depth discussion of leadership.

Performance. Organizations that want to move quickly through the phases of operational excellence need to ensure that their tactics are aligned with the strategy and overall direction of the organization. That means measuring only results that help drive the organization toward its stated goals. An activity that does not do that should be stopped. Organizations need to assess what employees are doing and ensure that all activities are adding value. If the strategy changes, the tactics need to change with it. It's amazing but true that many organizations change their future goals and direction but still operate the same way they did before. I tackle the challenge of focusing on performance in Chapter 5.

THE FOUR PHASES OF OPERATIONAL EXCELLENCE

As they work toward operational excellence, companies can progress through the four phases; the ultimate goal is reaching the fourth phase, which is mastery. Let's look at each phase.

Figure 2-3 outlines the progression to mastery.

Figure 2-3. The Four Phases of Operational Excellence

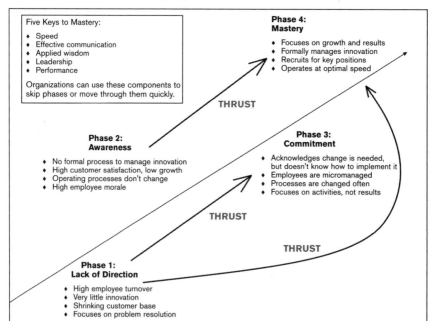

Phase 1: Lack of Direction

An organization in this first phase doesn't even know the importance of operational excellence. Such organizations tend to spend most of their time resolving problems as they arise (sometimes called "putting out fires") because they have not established a clear objective or future vision. Here are some characteristics of organizations stuck in phase 1:

- They have high employee turnover. Employees are not given the opportunity to take on new challenges and are not rewarded for their contributions, so they leave.

- They do very little innovating. They sell the same products and services they have always sold, using the same methods, and they try to sell them to the same customers.

- They move slowly. Decision making takes too long, and the organization is unable to take advantage of opportunities.

- Their customer base is shrinking. They try to sell the same old products and services to the same customers.

- Their processes have not changed. Organizations stuck in phase 1 don't review the way they operate to see if it is still appropriate for the market around them. They are stuck in the we-have-always-done-it-that-way syndrome.

- Rather than measuring results, they measure success by activity completion, but often those activities don't lead to results. They can't align activities with the future vision of the organization because they haven't identified what that vision is.

- They focus on resolving problems, not on taking advantage of opportunities. Because of that focus, they will be able to restore themselves only to past performance; they won't achieve better results.

Yahoo is a good example of a company that has had a lack of

direction for many years. Once dominant in its marketplace, Yahoo lost direction. It is trying to move out of this phase of declining performance through a string of recent acquisitions in the hope of becoming more relevant.

Phase 2: Awareness

Organizations in phase 2 are aware of the importance of operational excellence, but they are not sure what to do about it. They support the idea of looking at how they operate and tend to try many different initiatives, but many of those initiatives are not successful due to a lack of effective execution. Companies in phase 2 have some, if not all, of these characteristics:

◆ They have a clear strategic direction but are not sure how to align daily tactics with that vision. Activities that are not aligned often do not add value to the organization.

◆ Employees love working for the organization even though it is not as successful as it should be. Employees will tolerate a lack of success because of the comfortable work environment.

◆ Employees take initiative to make changes on their own, and these changes often yield a small benefit. However, there is no coordinated effort to mount initiatives that would drive a larger impact.

◆ A tremendous number of innovative ideas are identified, but there is no process to prioritize them and work on the ones that can have the most impact.

◆ The organization moves quickly but sometimes too quickly. There is little recognition that sometimes an organization needs to slow down in order to get better results.

◆ The organization is slowly expanding its customer base but stays away from any radical changes. Employees' skills are updated through training, and there is recognition that new skills are required.

♦ Customer satisfaction is high, but that doesn't usually lead to new customers or an increase in sales.

♦ The operations of the organization usually can't keep up with any rapid sales growth that occurs.

Many small businesses that grow quickly into midsized organizations find themselves stuck in phase 2. They grow at a rapid rate but want to still maintain the family atmosphere that was established when they were small. Often the company is still run by the original owners and founders, who are resistant to any change that might disrupt the culture they are so proud of. The organization gets comfortable, sometimes too comfortable, and is not prepared to make the changes required now that they have significantly increased in size.

Phase 3: Commitment

Organizations in phase 3 have started to implement a culture of operational excellence and are constantly looking to improve the way they operate. They are committed to making changes; their limitation is that they don't know the proper changes to make and instead rely on external factors to drive necessary changes. Those external factors can include a dependence on legislated change, a heavy reliance on external advisers, or bringing in temporary resources to support key initiatives. Without those external drivers, they tend to lose focus or slide back to old ways of thinking and doing business. Organizations in phase 3 have these characteristics:

♦ They try to align their tactics with the corporate strategy but need constant reminders to keep tactics and strategy aligned.

♦ They acknowledge the need to change the way they

operate but don't know how to go about making the changes.

♦ They often move quickly but can easily get bogged down in consensus building when it's not necessary, which slows them down.

♦ Employees are told they are empowered to make decisions, but management often intervenes and even micromanages.

♦ The hiring and retention strategy stresses the recruitment of specific people for key positions but is focused on skills and experience, not on expected outcomes and results.

♦ The organization measures success in a standard way but measures too many things to focus effectively on the key indicators.

♦ The organization does an effective job of acquiring new customers but often latches on to the latest sales trend to achieve a short-term boost.

Phase 4: Mastery

The fourth and final phase is mastery. Organizations that operate in this phase know what they need to do and have been able to internalize that knowledge to get consistent results. Organizations in this phase are often industry leaders that consistently perform at a high level. These organizations also know they can never allow themselves to stop improving, so they are never satisfied with the status quo. Here are some characteristics of organizations that have mastered the concept of operational excellence:

♦ The hiring strategy stresses the recruitment of specific individuals for key roles and focuses on outcomes and results, not on activities.

◆ The organization formally manages relationships with key customers, suppliers, and other business partners.

◆ The organization has developed key measurements that focus on growth and results, not just on the completion of activities.

◆ The organization has a formal process for managing innovation and the identification, prioritization, and implementation of new ideas.

◆ The organization optimizes speed; it knows when to move faster and when to move slower to maximize results.

◆ The organization provides unique ways to engage its customer base and uses current customers as a source of referrals to new prospective customers.

◆ The organization knows that strategy is organic; it is flexible enough to update its strategy as factors change.

◆ The organization recognizes the value of gaining an outside perspective; it utilizes outside advisers to help achieve its loftiest goals.

◆ The organization has a succession plan for key roles— which means not just the executive team at the top—and it provides growth and development opportunities for key future leaders.

◆ The organization is able to find performance boosts and money in areas where its competitors don't normally look (more about this in Chapter 5).

McDonald's is a great example of a company that is in phase 4. It takes a consistent approach with all of its restaurants and has developed an operational guide to ensure that the customer experience is the same regardless of where they are in the world.

McDonald's put a heavy focus on training employees and providing them with opportunities to grow and move up in the organization. Most McDonald's senior executives have risen from the ranks; many started working in an individual McDonald's store, often at the entry level.

The corporation takes industry-leading positions on safety and quality, gives back significantly to local communities, and has a clearly aligned strategy.

Remember, I use these four phases only to assess where an organization currently resides. These are not meant to label an organization or criticize them. You can move forward only if you know where you are starting from. Go back to Figure 2-3, and determine which phase your organization is in. (For a more comprehensive assessment, take a look at the Appendix.)

The good news is that organizations can move through the different phases quickly and even skip phases if they implement the right strategies and execute them successfully (I call these *operational thrusts*.)

Most organizations tend to start at the first phase and then move through the other phases sequentially, which is not necessary. As shown in Figure 2-3, an organization can move from phase 1 to phase 4 by focusing on the right strategies and implementing them successfully. The most successful companies can jump over steps, hit them all at once, or even do them in parallel. If an organization ties its approach to the five key elements required for mastery, it can accelerate its way through the phases.

CREATING GATES: PROTECTING YOUR GAINS

Once an organization has reached mastery, operational excellence becomes second nature: The culture is focused on driving the best possible results by constantly improving how the organization operates.

However, when you have achieved mastery, your work is not done. You need to implement gates, or backstops, to ensure that you continue to move forward and do not slide back into one of the previous phases. These gates can be different for each organ-

ization, but it is impor-
tant to put them in
place and to use them.

As a solo consultant
running my own organi-
zation, it is sometimes
difficult for me to main-

Your organization can use speed, effective communication, applied wisdom, leadership, and performance to give it an operational thrust through the various phases.

tain the proper mind-set when meeting with prospective clients. Like any business, mine has ups and downs, and the key to success is having the same mind-set regardless of the situation. I know that if I always have the best interest of my clients in mind (what I call "putting more food on my client's table"), and if I focus on working with organizations that I know can achieve significant value by partnering with me, then everyone involved will be happy.

I have created a gate for myself to ensure that I don't get too frustrated by specific situations. I create more intellectual property. Whenever I am feeling frustrated with the outcome of a situation, or if a client is not implementing what we had discussed, or if a prospective client has not returned my call, instead of getting frustrated, I create something. I write an article. I shoot a short video. I create something new that I can share with the people in my network. It has now become automatic for me: As soon as I feel frustrated, I create something. This keeps me in the right frame of mind to talk to the next prospect or the next client.

Here are some examples of gates you can use to stop from slipping backward from the phases identified earlier:

♦ Hold an innovation competition within your organization. Ask for ideas for improvement from employees, customers, suppliers, and other business partners. Hand out awards for the best ideas. This focus on quality innovation will generate an influx of new ideas that can help improve performance and force you to find a formal way of evaluating and managing them.

- ◆ Have a third party interview some of your key customers and suppliers to identify why they like working with your organization and what could be improved. This will give you some insights on what you need to keep doing to be successful and what you need to improve on.

- ◆ Ask your existing customer base for referrals to prospective new customers. This will provide you with leads to follow up with and gives you a reason to have additional conversations with current customers.

- ◆ Perform a review of a key department in your organization and look for gaps in the process or in the method of communication. Odds are you will find some opportunities to improve the way you operate.

The key is to use these gates as a way to continue to push forward. Establish a formal process so that when your organization experiences a difficulty, the setback triggers the use of one of these gates and your forward progress continues. This ensures that you won't slip backward, as so many organizations do.

Now let's look at four types of organizations and how they can use gates to maintain their success. Some of these organizations realized this in time to save themselves, but others didn't.

FOUR TYPES OF ORGANIZATIONS

Here are four scenarios of what can happen to organizations once they have achieved mastery in operational excellence. Not all the news is good, which stresses the point that, once it has achieved mastery, an organization still needs to work hard to sustain it.

Reaching Mastery and Staying There

McDonald's is a great example of an organization that is consistently in phase 4 and has mastered the key elements of operational excellence. For years, McDonald's has been the top fast-food chain in the world, staving off competition from many different companies. It has managed to do this while not only increasing its customer base but also by adapting its food offerings to changing customer demands.

McDonald's regularly changes its menu options to appeal to the needs and wants of new customers, while maintaining some of the staple options that appeal to the existing customer base. It has upgraded its restaurant locations to provide a more comfortable environment and has shed the image of cheap food and facilities.

McDonald's has been able to successfully adapt to the changing food industry and to a changing customer base, while continuing to develop and produce talented employees who stay very loyal to the organization.

Reaching Mastery, Then Losing Significant Market Share

Most of you will remember the Internet browser Netscape. Netscape was the first company to dominate the Internet browser industry. In the mid-1990s, Netscape had a market share of more than 90 percent in its industry. By 2006, it had less than 1 percent; as of 2008, the Netscape Internet browser was no longer supported by AOL (AOL purchased Netscape for roughly $10 billion in 1998). What happened?

Put simply, Netscape lost focus. As Microsoft, which was giving its browser away for free with its Windows operating system, threatened to take over market share, Netscape began to release additional features to its browser technology. The problem was that those features didn't work very well. Netscape focused on features, not on functionality, so customers began losing faith in its technology. Since Windows was already installed on most computers, and Internet Explorer (Microsoft's Internet browser) was comparable to Netscape's product, customers began switching en masse.

Netscape didn't have gates installed to stop this from happening. As many organizations do when they are in a dominant market position, Netscape believed its success would continue if it stayed the course and continued to release more bells and whistles. It realized too late the threat that Microsoft posed to its core business, and it underestimated the resources Microsoft was able to throw at unseating the industry leader.

Reaching Mastery, Then Disappearing

Blockbuster Video used to be one of the most popular places to rent movies and video games. It had significant market share and was poised for even greater success as movie theaters become more expensive, as more people were staying home to rent movies, and as video games from companies like Sony and Nintendo became more popular.

But Blockbuster lost touch with its customers and the direction of the market. The Internet increasingly became a source for entertainment (streaming and downloading), and cable companies latched onto customers' desire for immediate gratification. Netflix started up, first giving people the ability to have DVDs delivered right to their front door, then giving them the ability to rent and watch movies online through streaming video, without requiring any new hardware. The cable companies also started on-demand services, and customers could order movies directly through their cable boxes.

These new competitors put Blockbuster out of business. Why should people come into its stores when they could obtain the same movies without having to leave home? Blockbuster didn't have any gates in place to help it drive forward. If it had, it would have recognized the direction in which its customers were moving much sooner and would have been able to capitalize on it, as Netflix did.

Reaching Mastery, Losing It, Then Reappearing Even Stronger

IBM is a great example of an organization that had had a dominant position, lost it, and then regained it. IBM formerly dominated the personal computer industry. It built one of the first computers and some of the most powerful ones in the world. For a while, IBM was really the only player in the personal computer space. But it lost focus and lost touch with the customer and had to sell off its personal computer division to Lenovo in the early 2000s.

This was quite a blow for the company that had dominated the personal computer industry for so long. But they were too late in realizing that customers wanted more choice in the configuration of their computers, at the same time wanting them to cost less. So IBM lost market share to customized Dell computers and less expensive Compaq models. But, as other great companies have done, IBM used this major challenge as an opportunity to reinvent itself as a services company.

IBM has had a resurgence and is now in a better position than ever, albeit in a different industry altogether. IBM realized that its success would be in providing services to large companies—not only technology services but also consulting services and access to tremendously valuable data.

Under Lou Gerstner and Sam Palmisano, IBM completely changed the focus of the entire organization to a services-oriented culture. It moved from selling hardware and servers to selling solutions, advice, and partnerships with customers. IBM was able to do this because of the gates it had implemented that allowed it to change how it operated without sacrificing the quality of what it was providing to customers.

REDEFINING THE WAY WE MEASURE SUCCESS

Once we have determined that we need to implement ways to stop from backsliding once we've made gains in our pursuit of operational excellence, we need to implement measurements that align with that mind-set. The standard ways of measuring performance will no longer drive us toward growth and success.

Chapter 5 will cover this in more detail, but some key points are worth noting here.

Organizations tend to measure the same metrics they always have. Productivity, efficiency, customer satisfaction, employee morale, and profitability are all metrics that organizations use to show success. These are not wrong indicators, but they don't all motivate us to improve how we operate.

What does productivity really tell us? There are many different interpretations, but I'm sure of some things. It should tell us we are making efficient use of resources, but what are those resources work-

> **Great organizations have not only a clear vision of where they want to be but also the ability to change that vision and anticipate market changes.**

ing on? It's one thing to be busy; it's another thing to be busy working on activities that lead to increased growth. Again, we need to measure outcomes, not activities.

What about customer satisfaction? What does that really mean? Having satisfied customers doesn't mean that they will become ambassadors for our brand or refer prospective new customers to us or buy more of our products. High customer satisfaction scores mean only that an organization has met the expectations of its customers. Maybe those expectations were too low. Should we be patting ourselves on the back for meeting, or even exceeding, low expectations?

Organizations need to redefine the way they measure success if they want to thrive in the future. Figure 2-4 presents a comparison of old and new ways of measuring success. (We will spend more time on it in Chapter 11.) The first column of Figure 2-4 lists metrics used in the old way of thinking about operational excellence; the second column shows new ways of thinking—how organizations *should* be measuring success. These new ways of thinking focus on outcomes, not on activities. We need to redefine the leading indicators we use for benchmarking and measuring success.

Figure 2-4. The Future of Operational Excellence: Redefining How We Measure Success

Old Thinking	New Thinking
◆ Efficiency	◆ Effectiveness
• Productivity	◆ Performance boost
• Savings	◆ Growth
• Eliminating waste	◆ Driving innovation
• Standardization	◆ Customization
• Top-down change	◆ Engagement and empowerment
• Moving faster	◆ Optimizing speed
• Discounts	◆ Value
• Hiring	◆ Recruiting
• Customer equality	◆ Customer stratification
• Strategy development	◆ Strategy execution
• Customer satisfaction	◆ Customer retention and referrals

Think of your organization as a living organism that needs certain elements in order to thrive. Instead of water, soil, and sunlight, your necessary elements are people, processes, technology, communication, leadership, metrics, and speed. You need to ensure that all these elements are present in your organization. The next few chapters break down many of the core components and strategies of operational excellence, providing practical ways to improve the performance of your organization in key areas.

CHAPTER 3

ATTRACTING AND RETAINING TOP TALENT: DON'T SETTLE FOR SECOND BEST

WE TEND TO THINK OF OPERATIONAL EXCELLENCE in terms of production lines and logistics. We rarely think about how it pertains to people and leadership. That's why *attracting and retaining top talent* is one of the four core components of my redefinition of operational excellence.

I place it first in my list of the four components because it is what an organization must do if it is to innovate and collaborate, align strategy and tactics, and acquire and keep the customers it wants.

We often hear that people are the backbone of an organization and are essential to its success. But how do we put that principle into practice? What can we do to ensure that we have the right people working in our organization? The concept is simple: We need to put in place processes that help us attract and hire the best people.

But it's not enough to just bring in the best people. We need to keep them as well. We need to develop equally effective strategies to retain our best people and make them feel as though they are owners in our businesses. We need to create a culture where employees feel comfortable, feel appreciated, and feel their ideas are being heard.

Leadership is an important component of that, but not just leadership at the top. The best organizations encourage leadership at all levels. Let's delve into some important strategies to help ensure you have the right people in your organization to leverage all the opportunities that are out there for the taking.

First, though, here are my thoughts about what great leadership means.

THE KEY PRINCIPLES OF LEADERSHIP

As with any other concept or idea, leadership plays an important role in operational excellence. And both leadership and operational excellence need to exist across the entire organization. Organizations that are successful in improving results through operational excellence recognize that they need leaders at all levels in order to maximize performance and profits.

Strong leadership from the top is important, but it is also essential to have great leaders throughout the organization and to groom those leaders for future management roles.

What is the sign of a great leader? Too often, we evaluate leaders on the amount of money they make or their company's stock price. Although that information is important to consider, those factors alone don't make a great leader. In fact, those can be misleading indicators of how successful a leader is because they are only financial factors. If we used only those indicators to identify a successful leader, we would be missing the point of leadership. We don't want to imply that a great leader must make a lot of money or be a part of a money-making organization. Leaders can come in many shapes and forms.

How can we judge money-making leaders when the stock

market crashes? How do we judge leaders in government and not-for-profit organizations? Can a high school basketball coach be a great leader? Of course he can. The true test and measure of a great leader is one who motivates, inspires, and gets results during the toughest of times.

Four principles of leadership are always important, and they become even more important during tough economic and social times. The principles, in no particular order, are:

1. Communication

2. Inspiration

3. Determination

4. Accountability

Communication

Many organizations experience problems that are based in poor communication. Employees, suppliers, and customers need to know what is going on in the organization and want to know how the organization is going to make it through both the tough times and the good times.

There is a much greater risk of employees leaving an organization when they start to hear rumors of layoffs, takeovers, bankruptcy, and the like, while the leaders of the organization remain silent. Especially in tough times, leaders must have the integrity to be honest with their employees, even if doing so is difficult. Nobody wants to be the bearer of bad news.

With effective communication, leaders can help employees feel like part of the organization and accountable for making it a success. Employees may have a sense of betrayal when they hear gossip and rumors; whatever their response to the bad news that the boss conveys directly, they will not feel betrayed.

It is imperative that strategic decisions be communicated to the entire organization and that employees have a mechanism for providing feedback and suggestions. This communication can be accomplished through town hall meetings, e-mail updates from the president or CEO, a suggestion box, and so on.

Great leaders have a plan for communication at the ready and always err on the side of overcommunication; it is easier to scale back on the amount of communication than it is to compensate for insufficient communication. If you undercommunicate, the opportunity to involve employees has been lost and will be very difficult to recover.

It is also very important for leaders to know what to communicate. Here are some practical examples:

◆ If the company is going through tough times, communicate to employees the company's strategy for getting through the challenges and how the employees will be involved.

◆ If the company has a high turnover rate, let employees know what the retention strategy is going to be.

◆ If the company is going through a battle with a union, keep employees updated on the progress and maintain a positive attitude.

The key to communication is not only to do it early and often but also to do it effectively. Employees know that news will not always be good, but it's better for them to hear the news from the leaders of their organization than from the newspaper or from their customers. Developing and executing a communication plan can save an organization from a lot of issues down the road.

Inspiration

Inspiration can sometimes be an overused term, but the truth is that it takes a great leader to inspire an organization when economic challenges abound or when a new strategy is being implemented. Leaders may need to inspire employees to perform better, to be patient, or, in extreme conditions, even to show up for work the next day.

Leaders who lead by example will get the best results. Their motto should be, "Never ask someone to do something that I would not do myself." Of course, I am not suggesting that all leaders should circulate through the organization taking on every job, but if employees know you are willing to do whatever it takes to succeed, they will follow.

Inspiration can take many forms—from motivating people to be more productive to cutting travel costs. The key result is getting employees to support the direction of the organization. Even economic downturns bring opportunities for growth. If an organization is to take advantage of those opportunities, employees need to be on board and inspired that the organization is going in the right direction.

Great leaders need to stay flexible and able to adapt to challenges as they occur. They need to be able to find creative solutions to common problems and sometimes to go against the tide and take educated risks. Leaders who truly believe in their decisions and who can communicate that belief effectively will inspire others to believe as well.

Determination

Great leaders have a determination and a discipline to make things better, no matter what challenge is thrown at them. They do not jump ship as it starts to sink; they batten down the hatches and get ready for a fight.

There is a phrase that athletes use: "Leave it all out on the field (or the ice)." This is what great leaders need to do. They need to do everything they can to turn around the fortunes of the organization, with no regrets. Whether it's taking educated risks or making tough decisions, leaders who leave it all on the field give the game everything they have in order to make a difference.

In 2008, the board of directors of General Motors fully

endorsed and supported the work that its president, Rick Wagoner, had been doing. Even through significant layoffs, loss of market share, and low morale, Wagoner was determined to do what needed to be done for the business. The board supported him, saying that no one could have done a better job, given the circumstances. General Motors eventually got through the tough times and became more successful because its leader was able to make tough decisions in a tough environment.

Accountability

When organizations are going through tough times, the accountability of leaders needs to come into focus. Strong leaders take responsibility for their actions and can therefore make others accountable as well.

The best leaders are those who are willing to share the praise for successes and take the responsibility for failures—admitting mistakes and being accountable for them. Too often companies experience terrible results, and their leaders get huge compensation packages; they refuse to take pay cuts or they receive huge bonus packages while employee salaries are being frozen or even reduced. This is not being accountable for your actions.

One of the greatest examples of taking accountability was when Lee Iacocca, then president of Chrysler, cut his annual salary to $1 until the company improved its financial success. His belief was that he could not ask his employees to make sacrifices for the company if he was not willing to do so himself. That is being accountable to the organization and to its employees for its success.

It's no coincidence that companies run by great leaders are also more likely to take advantage of the tough times and come through in a better position than where they started. Everyone can relate to the analogy of the stock market losing value. Some see a retreat in the market as a sign to sell everything before prices fall even more, whereas others view a downturn as an opportunity to buy at a lower price. Which way do you see it?

THE FOUR ATTRIBUTES OF A GREAT LEADER

What attributes do all great leaders need to possess, regardless of where they are in an organization? Leaders should exist throughout an organization and be given the opportunity to shine. When you are assessing leaders and potential leaders within your organization to determine who has the goods, you can use these attributes as a guide for greatness. Insist on the following four attributes in people who constantly achieve great results, and you have found the leaders of the future.

Adaptability. Leaders must be able to lead in varying environments—a crisis, a financial boom, times of moderate success, or even ambiguity. Leaders must be able to understand and then adapt to the environment, including being able to tailor their leadership to particular circumstances or environments. Various groups and individuals may react differently in similar or even identical circumstances; a great leader needs to know how to effectively lead based on those varied reactions. Not all employees react the same way to a leader's style; great leaders need to know their people and how to help them be successful by developing strategies to which they will respond the most effectively.

Perceptiveness. Leaders must know what is going on around them, including the personalities of the people and teams they lead, the different agendas people have, and how others perceive the organization's leadership. Leaders must then use that information to determine how best to achieve the organization's goals and objectives. Analyzing the environment to develop and execute effective communication strategies is the sign that a leader is in tune with his or her surroundings.

Decisiveness. A leader needs to balance the desire for consensus with quick decision making. Great leaders know when they need to make a quick decision and when they need to spend additional time gaining support from others, all the while knowing that in most cases, some action is better than none. Leaders who excel don't shy away from these situations; they thrive on them. They can quickly decipher an effective decision-making style and act on it.

Humility. Great leaders give most of the credit to the people around them when things go well but shoulder most of the blame when things go awry. Smart leaders recognize that they need to be surrounded by smart people; they know that they can't do everything on their own and that people need recognition for a job well done. One of the sure ways to frustrate employees is for a leader to take credit for their work. Great leaders don't need to feed their egos by gaining praise. They are more satisfied when other people in the organization receive that praise. Humility in leaders inspires people to follow happily and productively.

Great leaders aren't always at the top of their organizations. Do you know who those people are in your organization?

> If you want to become a great leader, work on being adaptable, perceptive, decisive, and humble. Remember: Many of the great leaders in an organization aren't in the executive suite.

Is Leadership Innate?

Can leadership be learned or is innate? Let me settle that debate right now—leadership can be learned. It is that simple. People can improve the way they lead. Here are some ways that leadership can be learned.

Watch What Others Do. Think of people you consider great leaders and observe how they lead. How do they treat others? How do they make decisions? Observe what they do and what you can learn from them. Recognize that you will likely learn as much from watching poor leaders as you will from successful ones because they will show you how *not* to lead.

Be True to Yourself. This sounds corny, but you can't force a certain leadership style upon yourself, so find the style that works best for you. When you observe others, don't try to become them; instead, look for techniques and tools that you can incorporate into your personal leadership style—one that suits your personality and allows you to feel comfortable while you achieve dramatic results.

Focus on Strengths. Great leaders know what they do well, and they surround themselves with people who complement their skills and styles and are great at what they do. Great leaders don't try to be all things to all people. Recognize your strengths as a leader and build on them to improve your skills, while helping other potential leaders in your organization do the same.

I have seen people become great leaders by watching and learning and then developing their own leadership style. Unsuccessful leaders try to lead in a way that doesn't fit their personality. You can't force a certain leadership style; you need to develop a style that works best for you at the same time that you are learning from other successful leaders about how to get results.

Sam Palmisano and IBM

Sam Palmisano was president and CEO of IBM for ten years. During that time, he reestablished IBM as an industry leader and a standard-setting organization. The interesting part is that IBM essentially reinvented itself, reestablishing itself in different businesses than ones that they had had success with earlier. IBM has now become one of the leaders in data mining and consulting services, two areas they were not involved with when Palmisano took over. IBM even sold off its personal computer division in 2005.

Palmisano was able to accomplish this transformation through great leadership.

He realized that the future success of the organization was not going to be in selling hardware and computers, so he developed a clear vision of where he wanted IBM to go, which was to become involved in unique activities with high profit margins and the ability to constantly innovate.

He communicated this effectively to his organization and got everyone on board. He was decisive in the tactics that the organization needed to accomplish this goal. And he shared the success when it came.

Michael McCain and Maple Leaf Foods

In 2009, Maple Leaf Foods was linked to the deaths of 21 people in Canada due to a bacteria present in its popular luncheon meat products. Michael McCain, the CEO of Maple Leaf Foods, made many good decisions after the crisis hit and showed all the attributes of a great leader.

Imagine McCain's predicament. His food company was linked to multiple deaths as a result of the food that was produced in one of its plants. This disaster could have crippled the company. Instead, within a year Maple Leaf had regained much of its reputation and is still financially stable, although a little the worse for wear.

McCain took this terrible situation and used it to spearhead an initiative to increase the safety levels for all food manufacturers in Canada. When Maple Leaf assessed the damage and the reasons for the contamination, the company changed its internal safety and cleaning policies not only to meet government requirements but to significantly exceed them. Maple Leaf came out of this crisis as the champion of higher food safety standards in Canada.

So what did Mr. McCain do right as CEO of the organization? He made good decisions and exerted effective leadership:

+ He immediately and publicly took responsibility for the crisis and made himself accountable for resolving it.

+ He quickly developed a plan for dealing with the crisis, including identifying the root cause for the contamination and addressing it.

+ He publicly acknowledged the problem and publicly explained the steps the company was taking to resolve it—via television, radio, and YouTube.

+ He was transparent in his handling of questions and concerns and made himself available to reporters, regulators, and the families of the victims. He was never too busy to address concerns.

+ He became a champion for greater food safety standards for all companies across Canada.

This is what great leaders do: They accept accountability, they develop a plan to not only resolve an issue but to raise the bar for everyone else, and they communicate effectively and often. Michael McCain maintained those characteristics throughout the crisis.

ATTRACTING THE BEST PEOPLE

I've laid out a tidy framework for identifying, evaluating, and developing great leaders. Now all you need to do is to look for people in your organization who follow these principles and possess these attributes and then look outside your organization for such people and offer them positions with you.

How to do this and make sure your actions align with your pursuit of operational excellence? The key is knowing what you are looking for and then having the mechanisms in place to attract, hire, and retain people who have what you are looking for.

The key to success for any organization is attracting the right people. It's important to look for people who not only have the right skills but who also want to develop both personally and professionally. These traits help bring a level of accountability to the organization.

First, look at your organization to make sure it will be attractive to strong leaders. World-class organizations—the ones everyone wants to work for—have a few things in common. Here are some of those invaluable elements:

- People are respected for their ideas and talents.
- The majority of employees respect their bosses.
- Employees are encouraged and empowered to make decisions and use judgment.
- Employees see the part they play in the strategic direction of the company and know how they can help move the organization in that direction.
- Good performance is rewarded, and poor performance is not.
- Innovation and performance improvement are a part of the culture.
- Learning and development are encouraged, and employees have the opportunity to embrace new challenges and new roles.

People like working for Apple or McDonald's or Lululemon Athletica or Four Seasons Hotels for many reasons. Each of these organizations provides opportunities for employees to try new ideas, to move up within the organization, and to develop both personally and professionally. However, just because a company is a great place to work doesn't mean it will be successful, and just because a company is successful doesn't mean it is a great place to work. That said, the two often go hand in hand.

Here are four key strategies organizations can usefully employ to attract the best people.

Always Be on the Lookout

You never know when the best employees for your organization will present themselves, so you need always to have your eyes wide open for the opportunity. When you find people who are a great fit, hire them. If you don't have a specific role for them, create one. Talented people won't always fit into existing business models, but if you know they will be successful, create a position designed just for them.

> If you find a superstar, create a role, even if you don't have an opening. You can never have too much great talent.

Know Where to Look

Often organizations look in the wrong places for top talent. The first rule is that the most talented people are probably already working somewhere else. With the exception of students who are just out of school, the best people usually have jobs.

Determine how some of your current best people came to join your organization and then exploit that same path. Was it through referrals from other employees? Industry events? Did they come from your competitors or from outside the industry? Find out what has worked in the past, and replicate it.

An important tip: Often your most talented people will know of other talented people, so don't be afraid to ask them.

Know What to Offer

The most talented people aren't always attracted to the organization that offers them the most money. Money will definitely be a factor, but it's not the *only* factor. Find out what motivates your best people. Is it recognition? Status? Important projects?

Once you know what motivates your top people, you can leverage that factor to attract other top people.

Recruit, Don't Just Accept Applications

There is a time for hiring and a time for recruiting. The difference is that when an organization *recruits*, it is targeting a specific person or people, whereas *hiring* is when there is an open position and anyone can apply. Hiring (accepting applications) is fine for roles that require repetitive work or specific skills. You should use recruiting for the more strategic roles in your organization, especially ones with a high profile and high accountability.

Bringing in the Best People

Now that you have mastered the ability to attract the best people, you need to figure out which ones are right for you and bring them on board. The process can be easy and straightforward, or it can be difficult, especially when you identify talented individuals and don't have specific roles for them. Again, when you find a great talent, find a spot or create one.

The three attributes you should look for in any new employee are attitude, competence, and mind-set (I call these the "ACM attributes"). When your employees have the right mix of attitude, competence, and mind-set, you are able to maximize profitability.

Attitude. An employee with the right attitude has a passion for the organization and what it is trying to accomplish and is excited about being a part of that organization.

Competence. Competent employees have the skills and capabilities to do their jobs or the ability to learn the right skills.

Mind-Set. An employee with the proper mind-set recognizes the value of collaborating with peers and comes to work every day look-ing for ways to improve the performance of the company.

Figure 3-1 shows these three key attributes and how they need to intersect in order to maximize performance.

The Pitfalls of Ignoring the Key Attributes

If any of these attributes is missing, then the employee may not last very long with your organization. Integrate the search for these three attributes into your hiring process, and you will attract better people and make better hiring decisions.

Here's what can happen if one of these attributes is missing.

Silo Creation. When you have a combination of the right attitude and the right competence but the wrong mind-set, you encourage silo creation. A silo is created when someone focuses on his or her individual goals and accomplishments and doesn't appreciate the value of collaboration.

Figure 3-1. Key Attributes of Top Talent

1=**Silo Creation:** Right attitude and competency, wrong mind-set (some-one focused on their own individual goals and accomplishments).

2=**Talent drain:** Right competency and mind-set, wrong attitude (someone with no loyalty or passion for the organization).

3=**Poor results:** Right attitude and mind-set, wrong competency (someone who simply can't add value despite enthusiasm and being a good person).

4=**Profit maximization:** Right attitude, mind-set, and competency (someone who constantly adds value to the organization).

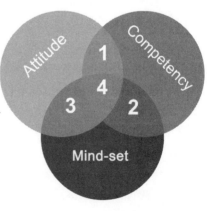

Talent Drain. People who exhibit the right competence and the right mind-set but the wrong attitude are not likely to stick with your organization. If an employee's attitude is misaligned, there will be no loyalty or passion for the organization; the person will find it easy to pull up stakes and move on. Even while such a person is with you, the lack of an emotional connection to the organization will make for a substandard performance.

Productivity Loss. A combination of the right attitude and the right mind-set but the wrong competence means a loss in effectiveness. People who love working for your organization but who don't have the skills required to be productive simply can't add much value, despite their enthusiasm and passion.

On the other hand, here's what can happen when you are at the intersection of the right attitude, the right competence, and the right mind-set.

Profit Maximization. Being there enables prospective employees to maximize their results for your organization and its people. You will have hired those who constantly add value to the organization, are passionate about the organization, recognize that collaboration with others can lead to better results, and want to share their success.

If you aren't hiring people with all three ACM attributes, then you will be putting in additional time and effort to finally hire the

> **Focus on attitude, competence, and mind-set to ensure that you bring the right people into your organization.**

right person. And I don't have to tell you the cost of frequent turnover, both financially and in morale. Integrate these attributes into your hiring process and retention activities, and your results will improve.

If you want to know whether you are well positioned in your efforts to attract the best people, ask yourself this question: "Are we a company that people line up to work for, or rush out the door to leave?"

Google is a great example of a company that uses a very rigorous hiring process to ensure that everyone it brings in will be a good fit for the organization. The hiring process consists of multiple interviews focused on problem-solving skills and the ability to react in various situations. Google needs people who thrive on ambiguity and on tackling impossible challenges that allow them to achieve results they never thought possible.

Google employees are empowered to make decisions because the organization is structured in small teams with big goals; thus it is essential to have the right people in those roles. Google offers many perks for employees—a high-end cafeteria, creative meeting spaces, an on-site gym, and so-called play areas—to ensure that employees stay productive and want to remain with the organization.

Google uses the same hiring strategy across the organization and in all the countries where it operates, allowing the company to maintain the culture it desires and achieve the expected results.

Contrast Google's success to what has happened with the CEO position at Hewlett-Packard over the last few years. First there was Mark Hurd, then Leo Apotheker, and now Meg Whitman—all hired within a period of three years. That is a lot of CEO turnover for an iconic company like HP.

Part of the reason for this turnover is the hiring process that HP used (or didn't use). Many of the members of the board of directors had never even met Leo Apotheker before he was hired. And many of them failed to realize what was needed in a new leader when he took over.

Aligning the leader with the direction of the organization is crucial. As we can see from Google's success, a rigorous hiring process is essential to ensure that the right people are being brought in at the right time.

Holding on to the Best People

Once you are able to attract and hire the best and brightest people to your organization, you need to keep them. There are a lot of misconceptions about the most effective ways to do this.

There are two key, underlying components to retaining top talent successfully: understanding their self-interest (what makes them tick) and implementing an effective recruitment and management process.

First, let's talk about understanding what is most important to your employees. Most studies cite the following as the key reasons people stay with an organization:

+ **Their Boss.** If people don't like working for their boss or manager, it will be difficult to maximize their performance and keep them with the organization.

+ **Respect.** Employees need acknowledgment that they are contributing to the organization and that their talents and hard work are appreciated.

+ **A Comfortable Work Environment and Culture.** Employees want to be excited about showing up for work every day; ensuring safety and a comfortable work environment is important to them.

+ **Coworkers.** The people we work with on a daily basis can have a huge impact on whether we stay with an organization. If we like working with the people around us, we feel an increased sense of accountability to perform and not to let them down.

+ **Intangible Benefits.** These intangible benefits can take the form of employee perks (on-site gym or high-end cafeteria) or working for a company with a great reputation.

+ **Money.** Notice that I'm listing this reason last. Money isn't often the reason that people stay with an organization. Top talent will be paid well wherever they go, so the preceding factors tend to be more important to them.

Here are some ways to maximize your ability to hold on to your top people.

Understand What a Top Performer Should Accomplish. Setting clear expectations for performance will go a long way toward making your top employees feel comfortable. Top people like to know what is expected of them, and they love the challenge of accomplishing goals that are a stretch. If they know what is expected of them, they can develop a plan to exceed your expectations and gain recognition.

Reward People for Achieving Results, Not Just Performing Activities. Your top people want to achieve great results, not just perform activities. Put measurements in place that focus on the achievement of results and outcomes, not the completion of activities.

Provide Growth Opportunities and a Comfortable Work Environment. Everyone wants to come to work in a comfortable environment. In addition, your best people want to be challenged. They want the opportunity to take leadership roles and work on exciting new initiatives. They even want the opportunity to fail as a way to improve and develop.

Understand the Wants and Desires of Your Top Performers. Work to understand what motivates your top performers—what drives them to better their performance and what they are passionate about—so that you can align your objectives with theirs.

Respect and Improve Skills and Work Performed. People want to feel respected at work and be acknowledged for their hard work. Set up award programs and events, and types of recognition.

Think even bigger when it comes to your best people. They likely don't want ribbons and trophies; they want the best and most challenging initiatives as well as high visibility across the organization.

Take Them to a Higher Level. Remember that your best people want to be challenged; they want to constantly develop and learn new skills. Help take them to the next level by giving them exciting learning and development opportunities. Give them the opportunity to improve on their strengths as leaders, and you watch them and the organization flourish.

A STRATEGY FOR TALENT MANAGEMENT

We've talked about who the best people are and how to attract, hire, and retain them. Now here are five things you can do to deepen the process of bringing in and keeping top performers.

Develop a Hiring Process That Maximizes the Number of Quality Candidates. Understand what you want your culture to be, what kind of people will fit into that culture, and what their accountabilities will be. Then hire only people who will fit into that culture. This is the ACM model discussed on page 59 in a nutshell.

Know Your Recruiting and Hiring Priorities. *Recruit* top people for the most important positions; in other words, target specific individuals for those key roles. Then *hire* for other positions in the organization through an application and interview process. In an ideal world, you do neither because the people you want seek you out.

Develop a Conflict Resolution Process. All organizations need to have a process by which any dispute with an employee can be resolved quickly. This means a firm understanding of who gets involved, when they get involved, and how that involvement should unfold.

Document Not Just Responsibilities but Accountabilities for Each Position. Most job descriptions focus on responsibilities, experience, and skills. Having clear accountabilities for the role sets expectations for performance; employees need to know what they are accountable for and how their success is going to be measured.

Find New Ways to Break Through Old Politics. Every organization has its share of politics, but politics should never be a hindrance to improving performance. Shake up reporting relationships, bring in new recruits, and try new ideas to break down the old barriers to success.

BREATHE LIFE INTO YOUR ORGANIZATION BY LETTING PEOPLE GO

"You're fired." We all laugh when we hear Donald Trump say those words, but in reality, firing someone is something we all dread doing. However, letting someone go can sometimes be just what your organization needs.

Can Employee Turnover Ever Be Too Low?

The short answer to that question is yes, employee turnover can be too low.

There can be a lot of discussion about what the right number is, but just as with an economy's unemployment rate, the turnover rate should never be zero or close to it. But doesn't this go against everything we've ever learned?

Having loyal employees who stay with an organization is not a bad thing, as long as they are growing with the organization and continuing to add value. Most organizations operate differently now compared to 15 or 20 or maybe even five years ago. Without new ideas and people who are able to adapt to a changing environment, companies will fall behind their competitors.

Letting go of underperforming employees is vital to the growth of your organization—and perhaps its very existence. Many times we know employees are not performing as well as they should be, but we are afraid to do anything about it. We send them to training classes, hire personal coaches, or find them mentors, and often none of that support works, probably because they are not the right fit for the job. You need to ask yourself whether they will ever be able to live up to their potential.

When the answer is no—when employees are underperforming—the result is stress for the employee, stress for the manager, and stress on the entire organization. It's just plain self-defeating for an organization to continue to employ someone who is not living up to expectations. Colleagues know when employees are not doing what is expected, and it frustrates them when nothing is done about it.

Approach letting someone go as an overall benefit to the organization. Here are some reasons why letting people go is often the best thing for your organization:

♦ Employees who do not meet or exceed expectations are replaced with people who can, so results improve.

♦ Your top people will see that there is no culture of entitlement. People need to continue to earn their positions.

♦ New employees bring new ideas and new energy into your company, as well as different perspectives; they can help challenge your established norms.

♦ Bringing new people on board gives the organization the opportunity to recreate its structure and the accountabilities of various job functions.

Letting someone go can be one of the toughest, most stressful things a manager has to do. But consider the negative impact on the morale of the rest of organization when you continue to employ someone who is a drag on your operation. Other employees will question your leadership if they know that people who are clearly underperforming are still in their jobs. When it is time to let someone go, do these five things:

Be Compassionate. The situation is not easy for anyone involved. Acknowledge that it is a difficult situation and treat the employee with dignity and respect.

Be Candid. Let the employee know why they are being let go; don't sugarcoat it. There can be no growth for them or for your organization if you offer excuses instead of being honest.

Be Concise and Succinct. Don't beat around the bush or launch into a long justification as to why the person is being let go. Get to the point and move on.

Provide Options. You may be able to provide the employee with support and the next steps. Perhaps you can offer them a position in a different department that's a better fit (but only if it is truly a better fit; don't just shuffle people around). Or you might set them up with career counseling or offer to introduce them to colleagues at other organizations that may be a better fit for them.

Recognize That This Is a Growth Opportunity. No one benefits when underperforming employees stay in their roles. Recognize that this is an opportunity to bring new life to the organization and to show other employees that they need to perform up to expectations.

Some employee turnover is healthy for an organization. But you must retain your key people.

Be strong, and know that each situation is different. You need to adjust to different circumstances and different personalities. Regard this as an opportunity to start anew and breathe new life into your organization. Remember Donald Trump. He repeats those two simple words and moves on.

IS YOUR TURNOVER RATE TOO HIGH?

Do you feel that your organization has a high turnover rate? Do you know what turnover is costing you every year? Most companies will answer yes to the first question and no to the second.

A high rate of employee turnover can be very costly. There are the costs of bringing in a new person for the role, the costs of any training that might be required for that new employee, and the costs of any severance package that might be owed to the employee who is leaving, just to name a few. And most organizations don't have a solid understanding of the underlying reasons people are resigning.

Being armed with reasons why employees leave your organization and the cost of that turnover makes you much more powerful; if nothing else, it motivates you to fix the problem. It is one thing to say, "We have had an average turnover rate of 12 percent in the past three years." It is much more powerful to say, "We have had an average turnover rate of 12 percent in the past three years. The main reason given was lack of employee engagement. That turnover has cost us more than $3 million per year." Which is the more actionable statement?

If you don't know how much employee turnover is costing your business or why people are leaving, then you can never fix the problem. Here are a couple of things you can do to get a handle on employee turnover:

Understand Why People Are Leaving. Perform exit interviews with departing staff and interview current staff to determine oft-cited reasons for resignations. Talk to people who used to work for the organization. It could be salary (although that's not the most likely culprit) or poor management or poor employee engagement. Whatever the main reasons turn out to be, knowing some facts will help put you on the right path for resolution.

Understand the Cost. It's important to understand how much you are spending on employee turnover. Tally the costs for hiring and training new employees, as well as the opportunity cost and lost productivity of having other employees fill in temporarily. These numbers will help raise the profile of the issue.

Once you can identify the reasons people are leaving your organization, you can start to develop a strategy for tackling the problem. Once you have a better sense of the most common reasons people are leaving, you need to plan how you will tackle them. If one issue tends to be management, then you need to look at how employees are being managed and the training offered to managers. If it is salaries, you need to look at your compensation structure. If it is the organizational culture, you need to decide on the culture you want and what you are doing or should be doing to put it in place.

When great people and top talent surround you, you can accomplish amazing things. Talented people push each other to ever higher limits. They are able to put their egos aside for the betterment of the organization and are willing to collaborate and share successes with their peers.

Mediocre people will get mediocre results. Remember that, when you envision what you want your organization to achieve, you can then take the rights steps to bring in the right people—the best people.

THE INNOVATION EQUATION: THE IMPORTANCE OF COLLABORATION

INNOVATION CAN BE GAME CHANGING and disruptive, but it can also be a small, incremental improvement to something that already exists. The key to innovation is progress. Generally, the progress that organizations make is forward, although sometimes organizations can progress by taking a couple of steps back, and there is nothing wrong with that.

Innovation keeps organizations alive and competitive. If an organization relies too heavily on what it already provides, eventually competitors will pass it by or customers will change what they are looking for.

The telephone is one of the most innovative inventions ever produced, and just look how it has evolved. Can you even fathom picking up an earpiece and speaking into a separate mouthpiece to an operator who then puts you through to another person?

Contemplate that notion while you talk and text on your mobile phone. Customer needs have changed, and the product we call the "telephone" has changed with them. (In the case of the telephone, the evolution of the product has made customers realize they have needs they never knew about before.)

Innovation is the improvement of an existing product or service to achieve a better outcome or the development of a new product or service that achieves a positive outcome. It can be a small improvement to something that exists, or it can disrupt an entire industry. That's what makes innovation so challenging and so fascinating. It is dynamic, constantly changing and moving. Organizations and individuals are constantly making improvements and conceiving new ideas.

There is no such thing as a status quo for an organization. You might think an organization can stagnate, but it can't. Even if an organization isn't making changes on its own, the external factors around it are changing. New competitors are entering and leaving the marketplace. Customer habits are changing. New legislation is being implemented. The economy is on an upswing or downswing. Organizations need to constantly adjust to those external factors by innovating. The best organizations anticipate changes and make adjustments quickly.

Innovation can be a small change to a process, or the development of a new tool, or the creation of a brand-new product. Innovation is not just about being stagnant or being satisfied with the status quo. Innovation is the difference between organizations that survive and those that thrive. And innovation, if it is to be effective in moving an organization toward operational excellence, must involve collaboration.

HOW TO FOSTER INNOVATION

Fostering innovation requires a certain mind-set to prevail, both within industries and within individual organizations. Figure 4-1 shows six attitudes and actions that are essential if an organization is to foster innovation.

Understand What Innovation Is

To foster innovation, we need to understand what it is. Innovation can be an incremental improvement or an enhancement to something that already exists; it can be a new, ground-breaking idea; or it can be anything in between. Innovation can take different forms even within an organization. Apple developed game-changing products with the iPod, the iPhone, and the iPad, but it has also made enhancements to existing products like the personal computer.

Incent Innovation

Organizations need to build systems that encourage and incent innovation. Incentives for innovation come not only from within individual organizations but also from governments, associations, and industry stakeholders. Organizations that successfully innovate provide incentives for new ideas and improvements, keep bar-

Figure 4-1. Attitudes and Actions That Foster Innovation

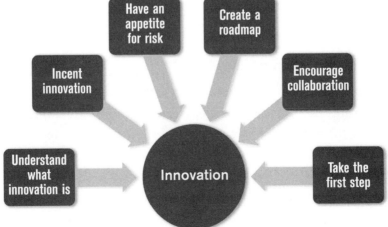

riers to innovation low, and provide funding for new and innovative ideas. Equally important is removing elements of the organization's culture that hinder or criticize those who are trying to innovate.

Have an Appetite for Risk

Innovation is a risky business; not all innovations are successful. For every successful product enhancement or new product that comes to market, hundreds have failed. However, with risk comes reward, so organizations that want to foster innovation also need to be driven by the prospect that great potential benefits can accrue from the innovations they are developing. Organizations need to encourage trial and error and positively acknowledge people, teams, and departments that are trying to fulfill a customer need or create one. Collaboration is key to encouraging this appetite for risk.

Create a Roadmap

As with any journey, the path to innovation needs a roadmap. When you plan a trip, a map shows you how to get from where you are to where you want to be. Innovation is no different. Once you have an idea of the direction you want to go, you need to develop a map that identifies the steps you need to take, the processes you need to follow, the stakeholders you need to engage, and the metrics you need to use to ensure you are successful in your journey.

Encourage Collaboration

Collaboration is an important component of innovation because innovation is not just about ideas; it is also about the implementation of those ideas. You can't expect to adopt new ideas without input and support from others. Those others might consist of fellow employees, customers, suppliers, investors, or other business partners. For innovation to be successful, some of the people most impacted by the innovation should be involved.

Take the First Step

Once you know the destination you want to reach and have created the roadmap to get there, you need to take the first step. The first step can be a difficult one, but without this fifth action, the first four are useless. You need to know where you are going, you need to have the appetite for risk, you need to have incentives to innovate, and you need to know what innovation means for you and your organization. Then you take the first step, and Newton's first law of motion takes over: "Something in motion tends to stay in motion."

Taking any step is often better than being stagnant. Remember that innovation can't happen in a vacuum, so it needs to be supported by many areas within an organization in order to be successful.

The Canadian bookstore chain, Indigo Books and Music, has had to rethink its business model; it needed either to innovate or to be left behind with the growth of digital publishing. Indigo Books and Music has transitioned from a bookstore to become more of a general store. It still sells thousands and thousands of books and magazines, but its product mix now includes a children's toy section, a section for music and DVDs, a section for household accessories (candles, vases, picture frames), and an in-store coffee shop. It also offers home delivery for most of its products.

Indigo Books and Music recognized that change was required. They defined what that change would look like for them and learned to understand innovation. They took a risk in trying to create a new model for bookstores and created a roadmap to get there. Every strategy they implemented moved them toward becoming a place for people to buy more of their household needs and spend more time in the store. They collaborated with customers and suppliers to find the right mix of products, constantly trying new product lines and removing others.

Indigo Books and Music has now turned its stores into meeting places where people come to browse, have coffee on their own or with friends, treat their children to a story hour, or sit quietly and read. They offer thousands of gift and household items that encourage customers to spend more time in the store. In a very challenging marketplace, Indigo Books and Music has evolved into not just a place to buy but a place to read, congregate, and socialize.

THE CYCLE OF INNOVATION

Innovations are commonly thought of as something new and game changing. However, many innovations are improvements on something that already exists. For every invention like the iPod or the television, a faster car or a stronger material is being produced. All of these are innovations.

In his book *The Innovator's Dilemma*, Clayton Christensen classifies innovations into three types: *evolutionary innovations*, which improve a product in an existing market in ways that customers are expecting; *revolutionary innovations*, unexpected innovations that do not affect existing markets; and *disruptive innovations*, which create a new market by applying a different set of values that ultimately (and perhaps unexpectedly) overtakes an existing market.

Although this might help us to segment different types of innovation, what's more important is creating a culture of innovation within your organization. Christensen gives us some guidance on the different types of innovation, but we need to have the culture and the mind-set to make any type of innovation work.

I believe there are only two types of innovations: those that work and those that don't. And there are only two types of organizations: those that succeed and those that fail. Innovation and success are closely linked. The ones that innovate are often the ones that succeed.

Why are some organizations more successful than others at innovation? Is it because they have smarter people who have better ideas? No. Is it because they are blessed with a better set of circumstances? No. Some organizations are better than others because they implement a culture of innovation and manage the innovation process. And they recognize the importance of collaboration within that culture.

A successful organization is one that grows constantly by balancing innovation with operational excellence. It is one that integrates innovative thinking into its daily operations. It encourages risk and rewards good ideas, even when they don't work. It encourages employees to show up at work every morning and question how the organization operates. A successful organization is one that excels at turning new ideas into usable products and services for its customers.

At companies like Google and Apple, employees are encouraged to spend up to 20 percent of their work hours investigating new ideas and improvements, even if they have nothing to do with the employees' actual job responsibilities. Many great innovations have come from employees working on challenges during their free time. But this kind of formal initiative is not required in order to encourage and foster an innovative culture.

What separates truly innovative companies from those that just say they are innovating? There are two key factors.

The first is the size of the organization. Smaller organizations tend to innovate more, though some large organizations are exceptional innovators. Companies like 3M, Apple, and General Electric are leaders in innovation. But for every one of those companies, a plethora of other large organizations are not innovating at all. Smaller companies often compete against larger companies, and sometimes their only competitive advantage is the speed and delivery of new innovations, large and small.

The second key factor is a culture of innovation. This means an organization encourages new ideas, challenges the status quo, and is comfortable with failure. Groundbreaking drug treatments go through years of trials before they work successfully on humans. The Wright brothers failed hundreds of times before finally achieving flight. A culture of innovation is a mind-set, not a process or a methodology, and that mind-set starts at the top. How do you treat employees who make mistakes when they try to develop a new solution or solve a customer problem in a different way? The answer to this question alone will tell you whether you are fostering a culture of innovation.

Within that culture of innovation is a collaborative subculture. Successful organizations realize that innovation won't be successful if it happens in a vacuum, that it needs input from many different stakeholders. Although one person may come up with an original idea, that idea will never become a success without the work of others to test the idea, enhance it, and make it successful.

Figure 4-2 depicts the cycle of innovation and its six stages. Paying attention to these stages will help your organization become successful not only in identifying new ideas, but also in prioritizing them, implementing them, and integrating them into your company's operations. You must ingrain this cycle into the DNA of your organization.

Figure 4-2. The Cycle of Innovation

The different stages of the innovation cycle revolve around the empowerment of your employees.

Gather

Organizations must encourage a culture in which new ideas are generated and employees are encouraged to think of creative solutions and improvements in the way the company operates. The key at this stage is not to focus on details but to foster ideas. Encourage a company-wide brainstorm in which no idea is too far-fetched.

Hubspot develops inbound marketing software that helps companies attract new leads and turn those leads into new customers. Hubspot holds monthly "sprints," in which teams are organized around developers and product managers. These teams avoid detailed specifications and plans and instead focus on generating new ideas.

One of the keys to success in the gather stage is that these new ideas may come from employees, customers, suppliers, or other business partners. Collaborative discussions with your business partners can yield productive ideas, and you may get unexpected perspectives from people outside your organization.

Review

Ideas that are identified in the gather stage need to be reviewed for impact and usefulness. What this really means is that the risk of each idea needs to be assessed; you need to get at least a cursory understanding of the potential rewards. What will be the impact of the idea? What risks are associated with it? What is the level of effort required to implement the idea? All these questions need to be answered.

You can establish a review team, or the review can be done by one person. Each organization is different, but as a general rule, collaboration is a key factor in making innovation work: The more of the right people you can involve, the more ownership each idea will have.

Develop some parameters around how ideas are chosen for development. Then create a short list of those ideas that have the best potential for success, the highest potential impact, and a tolerable level of risk. Having guidelines for the selection process makes reviewing the ideas easier and more transparent and gives the review team the ability to focus on certain decision-making criteria.

Try to make the review a rich collaboration. It's important to involve representatives from different departments within the organization to ensure a broad consideration of each idea. You may even bring in representatives from outside the organization who can offer a different perspective on the discussion. This collaboration will help look at the idea from different angles and even enhance its viability.

Prioritize

Once all the ideas have been reviewed and a short list has been made, you need to examine the remaining ideas to identify those for which at least some progress is possible.

It's important to recognize from the outset that not all ideas are going to be addressed, so you need to establish how they will be prioritized and how that prioritization will be communicated to the organization as a whole. Will it be based on senior leaders making intuitive decisions, or will they use objective, transparent decision-making criteria? Do you move forward only if there is dramatic financial impact or, say, because it is the right thing to do for your customers?

The objective of prioritizing is to select one or two ideas that can have the greatest impact or that can provide the best results and then to move forward with only those.

Apple had the idea for the iPhone and the iPad at the same

time, but Steve Jobs decided to pursue the iPhone first because he wanted to change the way people interacted with their cell phones. Apple built the iPad only when they saw how poorly other tablets were being made.

It's important to prioritize, or nothing will get accomplished. When you have too many priorities, you end up with none.

Plan

Now that you have one or two ideas to move forward with, develop an execution plan for getting those ideas to market. Identify who will work on the idea, the timelines for completion, what success will look like, and who will be accountable for that success. This plan can then be tracked and measured to ensure that progress is being made.

Don't just track activities and tasks; focus on results and outcomes. Look at your plan and identify areas where things could get held up or sidetracked, then take measures to make sure that doesn't happen. Look at what has worked for your organization in the past, and replicate it. Look at other successful product launches, determine why they were successful, and repeat the process.

Organizations like Google plan their product releases very carefully in order to gain an advantage over the competition. They assign project managers to each release to ensure that accountability is sustained and activities are completed on time and successfully.

Execute

Begin executing the plan. This means assigning resources to the idea, along with clear roles and responsibilities; most important, things need to actually get done. Someone, whether a project sponsor or senior executive, must have overall accountability for the success of the initiative, and this should be clear to everyone involved.

The execute stage separates market leaders from the rest of the field. Those that can execute most effectively will dominate by combining speed and quality. For years, IBM dominated the personal computer industry. Due to a lack of execution of new ideas and a change in strategic direction, IBM no longer even makes personal computers. Toyota cars used to be synonymous with quality, but after the company grew too quickly and executed poorly, the brand's reputation and sales suffered.

It's also important to note that the better the collaboration you have had up to this point in the process, the easier execution will be. If the right people have been involved in the reviewing, prioritizing, and planning stages, then they will know what is expected of them and their criteria for success. That serves as a much better foundation for success than if you were just bringing them into the fold at this point.

Integrate

Ongoing execution and support for innovation needs to be integrated into the company's daily operations. This integration includes transitioning relevant knowledge and maintaining focus on which parts of the organization are accountable for the success of the innovation. After this step has been completed, the new idea should be fully integrated into your operations and your support functions.

At this point, do one final piece of integration: Review the success of the initiative, and integrate any lessons you've learned into your organization's way of operating. Identify what went well and should be repeated and what needs to be improved on in your company's innovation cycle so that it works more smoothly the next time you undertake something new.

> There are two keys to implementing a culture of innovation: Empower employees to try and fail, and formally manage the innovation process.

Managing Innovation

The empowerment that's at the heart of this cycle gives your employees the ability to make decisions, try new ideas, and collaborate with others. After the integration is complete, you can begin the cycle again, generating new ideas and innovations. If you have previously generated ideas you now want to act on, you may want to fast-track them to the prioritize stage.

Make sure that your company is constantly moving forward one step at a time. Too many organizations breathe in their own exhaust and become complacent after one or two successful initiatives. Focus on establishing a culture of innovation that will ensure your company's success for years to come, and focus on managing the cycle of innovation with each new idea. Even if a given idea is not a commercial success, your process of bringing that innovation to market will remain solid.

Innovation needs to be like a flowing river, constantly changing and moving and going in different directions. When the water stops flowing, a river becomes stagnant and dries up. The same stagnation can occur with your ideas and eventually your results if you don't figure out how to harness the power of your people and encourage them to take risks as you manage the innovation cycle.

Think of how the planets in our solar system revolve around the sun. Without the sun, none of the planets would survive. Similarly, without empowerment, innovation will not be sustainable. The successful completion of the innovation cycle depends on permitting your employees to fail productively.

Productive failure is a concept that many organizations have trouble embracing. It's hard to accept the fact that sometimes, in order to improve, you need to fail. Not every organization makes that connection, but it is evident throughout successful companies. The most successful companies recognize the value of a failure. They also recognize that there can be a problem not just with the failure in and of itself but with how people react to the failure. Do they hang their heads and sulk, or do they get energized because they are one step closer to making an idea viable? Successful companies foster the latter response. Also, failure can help an organization improve on and enhance the original design of the product or service. If it didn't work, why didn't it work? What enhancements can be made not only to fix it but to make it better? Failure provides organizations with the opportunity to develop better solutions.

Four Keys to a Successful Cycle of Innovation

Here's a quick summary of four actions you can take to effectively manage the innovation cycle:

- Be collaborative in the broadest sense. Encourage new ideas from all sources—customers, employees, suppliers, and other business partners. You never know where your next great idea will come from.

- Put a lot of attention and energy into assessing the risks and rewards of those ideas. If you decide to move forward with a new idea, then you should know why; you should be able to clearly identify any risks or issues associated with pursuing the idea.

- Prioritize based on key factors. Look for ideas that will have the largest impact on your business and a high potential for commercial success.

- Focus on effective planning and execution. Without execution, there is no strategy. Planning is useless if the plans are not executed. It's important to plan, but it's even more important to implement and execute effectively.

A CULTURE OF INNOVATION: THE INTERACTION OF EMPOWERMENT AND SKILL

Imagine an organization in which all of the employees come to work every day wanting to improve how the organization operates. The hallways buzz with collaborative discussions and new ideas. People are energized about the prospect of creating new solutions to problems. Every office and meeting room is a laboratory where employees try out ideas and solutions.

These organizations exist; they are all around us. They have created a culture that encourages, fosters, rewards, and even incents innovation.

The leadership of a company can't just state publicly that the company has an innovative culture. Every organization says that. What differentiates those that have an innovative culture and the ones that just say they do? Two things: empowerment and skill level.

Empowerment means that employees can make decisions they feel are in the best interest of the organization and its customers. Many decisions don't require executive approval, and employees are not reprimanded for making a "wrong" decision, as long as they learn from it. Great organizations understand that having a culture of innovation means that everything they do is a learning process. Every failure is the next step on the way to the next great product or service.

If you walk around the hallways of an organization with an innovative culture, the feeling is palpable. Employees are energized about new ideas and are constantly huddling to bounce ideas off each other. There are very few formal meetings. These formal meetings are replaced by informal collaborations in which employees from different departments are collaborating on an idea or a solution to a problem. If a new or different perspective is needed, the employees find the right person to provide that perspective.

The best companies recognize that without failure, there will be no successful innovation. The massive Tata Group gives an award each year for the best idea that failed. This actually encourages people to try out new ideas and supports employees even if they fail. According to Ratan Tata, chairman emeritus of the Tata Group, "Failure is a gold mine for a company." Do you embrace failure in your organization, or are you afraid of it?

Employees must have the ability and competence to do their jobs properly. Having the proper *skill level* means that people are capable or that they can learn how to be capable of meeting or exceeding the organization's standards and expectations. It also means that employees are in the right positions—ones that are a good fit and in which they are set up for success.

Figure 4-3 provides a diagnostic for empowerment and skill level and how they affect the innovation an organization is capable of. Where does your organization fit based on this conceptualization?

Figure 4-3. Diagnostic: Do You Have a Culture of Innovation?

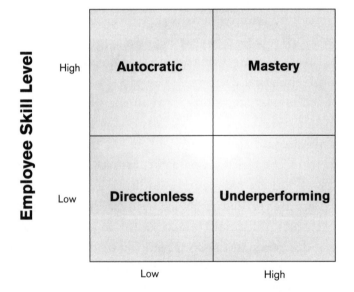

Directionless

If your organization is in the bottom-left quadrant—your employee skill level and employee empowerment are both low—your organization lacks direction. (To put it more positively, your organization has a great deal of opportunity for improvement.) Here are some of the characteristics of organizations in this quadrant:

- Employees don't have the power to make decisions; senior management must approve everything.

- Employees are not encouraged to bring new ideas forward; if they do, no one takes ownership or can act on those ideas.

- The organization is not very good at commercializing new ideas.

- It is ineffective in measuring success; in extreme cases, it has no metrics to show success in driving innovation.

- Employees don't collaborate with each other to develop their ideas.

- Employees do a lot of duplicated and failed work that adds no value to the organization.

Autocratic

If your organization is in the top-left quadrant—it has a high skill level but low empowerment—you are an autocratic organization. There is also a great deal of opportunity for improvement here, but senior management must loosen the reins on the organization. Organizations in this quadrant tend to have these characteristics:

- Senior management doesn't trust the employees to make the right decisions.

- The organization measures activities and tasks, not outcomes and results.

- Employees are frustrated because they are not included in key decisions.

- Communication is ineffective, and change is forced from the top down.

- Innovation is viewed as the responsibility of the senior management team and no one else.

- There is a lack of collaboration. Silos have been created across the organization.

Underperforming

If your organization has high empowerment but a low skill level, it falls in the bottom-right quadrant of the figure; it is underperforming. Again, there is opportunity here, but the organization needs to go out and hire the right people. Organizations that are underperforming have these characteristics:

- Employees make many wrong decisions and don't integrate what they've learned from failed innovations.

- Senior management is too far removed from daily tactics, and those tactics don't often align with the organizational strategy.

- The organization has tried many innovations that have failed; it is poor at commercializing innovation.

Mastery

If your organization is in the top-right quadrant—high empowerment and a high skill level—you are an innovation master. This is where all organizations should want to be. This is an innovative culture that provides the right level of empowerment for its employees. They take on the accountability for success and failure of their ideas, and they have the ability and skills to be successful. Here are some characteristics of organizations that are innovation masters:

- Employees can make decisions and try new solutions that they feel are in the best interest of the organization and its customers.

- Innovation is removed from the standard metrics of success that are used for the rest of the organization, which removes the focus on short-term results.

- The process of innovation is formally managed and measured.

- Employees are responsible and accountable for the success and failure of their ideas. They are given a challenge and told to go figure it out.

- Employees are given the ability to bring in whoever is necessary from within the organization to make the innovation more successful.

- Employees take on ownership for the solution and are self-motivated to make it the best solution possible.

- Innovation is funded separately from other initiatives in the organization.

HOW TO BECOME AN INNOVATION MASTER

We all want to become innovation masters. We all want our organizations to continuously grow and improve. We also need to remember that innovations can be small, incremental improvements. They don't all have to be game changers. What's important is that employees come to work every morning looking for ways to improve the performance of the company and that those employees are in roles in which they can be successful.

One of the strategies you can implement to help your employees become more empowered and accountable in innovating is to provide them with the critical thinking skills required to identify new opportunities. For example, you might develop two or three criteria that employees can use for assessing new opportunities or show-case some of the more successful innovations and highlight the process those innovations went through. Giving employ-ees this sort of support

Fostering innovation masterfully means funding it and measuring it differently from your daily operations. Encourage employees to generate and investigate new ideas that are not subject to scrutiny for short-term results.

will encourage them to take ownership of new ideas and show them what is possible.

As part of this process, senior management needs to let go of some control and give it to the employees. You will find that if, say, you develop innovation criteria and effectively communicate them across the organization, you will see more effective presentation of ideas. Employees now know what senior management considers a good idea.

One of my clients was having a real challenge getting new inno-vations implemented. The process of identifying the benefits and details of innovative ideas was taking several months. By the time the idea was fully developed, it would no longer be innovative, and they would abandon it. This is the process they would follow:

1. A division manager would take a new, innovative idea to the senior management team.

2. The senior management team would review the idea and provide comments to the division manager. Almost always included in those comments was that the division manager needed to work with the other division managers to identify any impact on their divisions as well as additional benefits.

3. The division manager would work with some of the other division managers to identify the impact and benefits and better develop the idea.

4. The idea would then come back to the senior management team for review.

What we realized in assessing this process was that not only was the organization wasting time and energy presenting underdeveloped ideas to senior management but that accountability and empowerment was lost when division managers were asked to collaborate with their peers. Meanwhile, division managers were measured, in general, on their own success, so they were incented to try to retain the benefits from any new ideas they developed. Therefore their ideas tended to focus on maximizing results for their division and ignoring the impact on others. As soon as the perceived benefits were reduced as a result of the impact on another division, the division managers would lose interest in moving the idea forward.

To eliminate these issues, we implemented an innovation process that encouraged collaboration and set reasonable expectations for the development of new ideas. Because the senior management team would review only ideas that had been reviewed by all the division managers, what was presented to them was a comprehensive view of the risks and rewards of the new innovation. We developed a framework so that all new ideas had to meet certain criteria; thus the presentation of the ideas was consistent.

Once these changes were made, the senior management team reviewed fewer ideas, but the ones they did see were likely to have a bigger impact on the organization. Division managers collaborated more because the measures for success were changed to encourage that collaboration; these new innovations were funded separately to remove the individual agendas and instead focus on what was best for the entire organization.

It's important to understand that effective collaboration is not about bringing in the maximum number of people possible; it's about bringing in the right people. Consider who could look at the innovation from a different perspective, and bring in those people, the ones who will add value to the process. Collaboration is about a commitment to work toward a common outcome. By encouraging this behavior, my client was able to focus on better ideas and, more importantly, implement them successfully because the key stakeholders were involved from the outset.

Creating a process to manage innovation is not that difficult. Frankly, most organizations are probably already doing it in an informal way, but they are most likely missing some important components. Earlier in the chapter, we discussed the cycle of innovation (Figure 4-2) and how it can help organizations manage the innovative process more formally. To maximize the effectiveness of this cycle of innovation, organizations should be asking themselves:

♦ Where are the innovative ideas coming from? Where should they come from? How many ideas should we be identifying every month?

♦ How do we evaluate the ideas to ensure that we move forward with the right ones? Who should be involved in the development of the idea and testing its viability?

♦ How do we know whether an idea was successful? How do we measure progress and success?

♦ What kind of a plan do we need to execute in order to turn good ideas into something commercially viable?

♦ How do we compare against our best competitors?

In a complex and interconnected world, organizations can't afford to miss any opportunity for an advantage. Managing innovation according to this process and asking the right questions may give you that advantage you need.

In a 2013 survey of 450 companies, the Conference Board of Canada found that more than half had no formal innovation process. How is that possible? In an age where innovation and growth are paramount to success, a significant number of organizations were not formally managing the innovation process.

Companies may wonder, "How do we know if our innovation process is successful?" The simple answer is that an organization needs to put metrics in place that show success. One way to know that your innovation process is successful is if customers are buying the products and services that result from that process. Instead of focusing on the number of new products and services you bring to market, measure the percentage of revenue those new products and services represent. An innovation can be successful only if it has commercial viability; otherwise, why innovate?

An organization can say that it has a culture of innovation only if a large percentage of its revenues come from products and services that didn't exist, say, five years ago. If you want to know whether your organization is successful at creating innovation, look at the breakdown of your revenue. How much of that revenue is represented by products and services that did not exist five years ago? If the answer is less than 30 percent, then you are not an innovative company.

How many new ideas have you brought to market successfully? How many improvements have you made internally that have had an external impact? You may be a successful company, but if you haven't made a significant financial contribution through new ideas and innovations, then you're not an innovative company.

ACCELERATING THE ADOPTION OF INNOVATION

When you have a new idea or enhancement, what can you do to accelerate the adoption of that innovation? Here are a few strategies.

Increase Collaboration

You can accelerate the adoption of innovation by collaborating on ideas with your suppliers, customers, and other business partners. Your suppliers have a unique perspective into your organization and may surprise you with their suggestions for how your organization can improve performance. There are many successful examples of organizations that have worked with their suppliers to tackle specific issues and opportunities and, as a result, developed new products and services.

Auto companies like Toyota and Honda work very closely with their suppliers to ensure that the parts the suppliers make are of the right quality and the right fit. Key suppliers are brought in early as a part of the design process, not only to ensure that they can support what is being designed but also to bring different perspectives to the discussion that can enhance the innovation.

Your customers also have a unique, yet different perspective on your organization; they are intimately acquainted with your products and services—they use them. Make sure you understand the customer viewpoint and integrate that into your innovation process. Collaboration with customers or clients is an untapped resource that organizations often ignore.

Many technology companies, like Apple and Dell, involve their customers in the development of new products. Involving the customer in the design process is a strategy that more and more organizations are employing. Not only does it help to create brand ambassadors (more on this in Chapter 6), but it also helps to ensure that the innovation will be commercially viable.

Remove Constraints

Removing the constraints that hinder innovation will go a long way in accelerating your organization's adoption rate of new products and processes.

Such constraints might be cultural, such as creating an environment in which failure is not tolerated. They might be based on poor measurements, such as evaluating new innovations in the same way that existing products and services are evaluated. They might be politically based; one individual or department may exert too much control over the direction of the company. They could be based on fear; some companies have had great success over the years and are afraid to change.

Whatever the constraints are, find them and remove them so your innovative culture can flourish.

Develop Tools

The development of tools can be an effective strategy in fostering innovation. We have discussed the cycle of innovation as a strategy for managing the innovation process. You can also develop criteria and guidelines to help make the assessment and prioritization of new ideas more consistent across the organization. You may even decide to develop an innovation template for the organization to follow as it identifies the potential costs and benefits of a new idea, as well as its risks and rewards.

Measure Appropriately

It's important to ensure that your organization is measuring the right success indicators. Cost savings may not be the most appropriate way to measure a new innovation. Measuring the number of ideas doesn't tell you whether you have any quality ideas, only that you may have a lot of ideas to review.

Look at measuring the percentage of company profits that came from products and services launched in the past three years. Look at the time it takes for customers to adopt your new innovations. Measure the impact that process improvements have on your bottom line. Those types of

To accelerate the adoption of innovation, increase collaboration, remove constraints, develop tools, and measure appropriately.

metrics will give you a better sense of how successful (or unsuccessful) your innovation process is.

Figure 4-4 identifies some of the key components in accelerating the adoption of innovation. As the figure illustrates, all the elements of the innovation process need to be aligned with a common goal. This doesn't mean that all the elements need to be aligned with each other in the solution, but they all need to align in their own way with the goal or outcome to be achieved. That common goal is what makes collaboration possible, and collaboration is what, in turn, allows an innovation to succeed.

Some Examples

Let's look at some specific examples of innovative ideas that companies are implementing. Remember: Innovation can take many forms, from a simple enhancement to an existing process to a game-changing invention.

Procter & Gamble Canada. This organization is constantly innovating. It removes innovation from the constraint of its daily metrics and thus unleashes its people to be creative. The organization encourages failure and funds innovation separately to foster its innovative culture. This is one of the key reasons P&G Canada has been an industry leader for so many years.

Revolution Foods. A food-service company that provides meals and nutrition education to schools across the United States, Revolution Foods uses locally produced food to support the communities it serves. The company employs some unique ways of innovating. It does a great deal of testing of new foods with the children who will be eating the meals each day (its customers); it sends nutritionists into each school to help with the adoption of new meal programs; and it provides nutrition education to the students.

Figure 4-4. Accelerating the Adoption of Innovation

India's World Health Partners. In delivering health and reproductive health services to rural and marginalized communities in the developing world, this organization uses innovative technology to link the informal health workers in remote villages with physicians in telemedicine networks that provide people in remote villages with the same level of care as someone in a larger community.

IDEO. Led by founder David Kelly, this well-known design firm innovates using a concept they call *design thinking*. According to IDEO's Web site, design thinking "brings together what is desirable from a human point of view with what is technologically feasible and economically viable." This might mean assembling a diverse group of people and watching them use products in order to figure out what people really want. This approach to innovation has led to some amazing new product designs, including the first Apple mouse and the Palm V PDA.

HMV Canada. This company operates more than 100 retail stores in

Canada, selling CDs, DVDs, and other audio and video recordings. It recently launched a digital music service called The Vault; users can sign up for a subscription-based service to stream music (and possibly eventually movies) or download them to a phone or mp3 player. At first glance, it might seem that this move would hurt their physical sales. But as HMV Canada president Nick Williams has said, "We absolutely believe we should provide people with music in any way they choose to experience it, whether that's [to] download, stream it ... or come into stores and buy it physically." This is a great example of innovating to meet new customer demands.

The Cable Telecommunications Industry. For years, this industry has been innovating to include an increasing number of services—cable TV, Internet services, telephone services—and build a large sub-scriber base. The approach was to sign up as many subscribers as possible and only then to worry about how to profit from those subscribers. Something very similar is taking place with social media companies like LinkedIn, Facebook, and Twitter. They are constantly providing new services and building a huge base of users. Once they have that massive user base, they will figure out how to make money from their users.

Think about some of these examples and where you found yourself on the culture of innovation diagnostic earlier in the chapter (Figure 4-3). Recognize that none of these innovations would be possible without collaboration, both internal and external. Bringing the right people together toward a common goal is the right formula for successfully managing and implementing innovation. Now come up with two or three things you are going to do to improve innovation within your organization.

CHAPTER 5

ALIGNING STRATEGY AND TACTICS TO ENHANCE PERFORMANCE

To take advantage of opportunities when you find them, your organization needs to align its strategy and tactics. Strategy is the *what* (what you want to achieve), and tactics are the *how* (how you will achieve it). Many organizations develop a great strategy but fail at the tactical execution stage, often because the activities the organization performs are not aligned with its strategy. In other words, how the organization tries to execute its strategy is not aligned with what it is trying to achieve.

Organizations need to tie their mission to their strategy, and then execute their strategy in their tactical operations.

Here's why it is essential to align your organization's strategy and the tactics employed to execute the strategy. When strategy and tactics are aligned:

♦ You ensure effectiveness of your resources, which are

focused only on activities that add value to your organization and customers.

♦ You eliminate the duplication of effort and gaps in accountability.

♦ You can measure success and results, not activity completion.

♦ You can respond quickly when activities are not helping to achieve your desired outcome.

♦ You have a clear roadmap to communicate both internally and externally.

♦ You increase your ability to attract and retain the best people.

♦ You elicit trust from your customers, leading to stronger loyalty because they can see the direction your organization is going—not through interpreting your lip service but by observing your actions.

Aligning strategy and tactics means that everyone in the organization not only knows the direction the organization wants to move; they also understand their specific roles in helping the organization get there. Too many organizations focus on the completion of activities, not on the achievement of results. And those activities are often not aligned with the future state the organization wants to achieve.

Consider the so-called customer-facing organization that contacts customers only when there is

> **Aligning strategy and tactics is not about activities on a project plan. It is about ensuring that employees know their roles and what is expected of them as the organization pursues its strategy.**

something new to sell. Or the entrepreneurial organization in which all decisions must be approved by the CEO. Or the company that preaches diversity yet has a management team who are all of the same ethnicity. These are all cases where strategy and tactics are not aligned.

Most organizations fail when implementing their strategy (in other words, their execution is poor) because they lose sight of where they want to be. They get caught up performing activities that do not move the organization closer to the desired state. They communicate their vision poorly, and they lack accountability.

Here are a few key success factors to consider when aligning strategy with tactics:

- Organizations need to understand and effectively communicate the desired future state.
- They need to perform activities that move the organization closer to that future state.
- They need to establish accountabilities and performance measures that align with the desired outcome.
- They need to ensure that everyone in the organization understands his or her role and accountability in achieving that future state.

WITHOUT EXECUTION, THERE IS NO STRATEGY

Aligning your strategy and tactics is important, but you also need to become experts at execution. Executing effectively on your strategy and plan is what differentiates the great organizations from everyone else. Great organizations are able to make things happen quickly and effectively. They are able to turn ideas into commercially viable products. They can turn opportunities into profit increases. They can turn words on paper into results.

Mastering strategy execution requires equilibrium among three components: prioritization, accountability, and harmonization. The numbers 1 through 4 in Figure 5-1 show what happens when these three components intersect.

Figure 5-1. Mastering Strategy Execution

1= **Unclear vision:** the activities being worked on and the accountability for success don't align with the future vision.

2= **Wasted effort:** the accountabilities align with the future vision, but there is no determination of the most important activities to acheive that vision.

3= **Poor results:** the activities align with the future vision, but there is no accountability for results.

4= **Execution excellence.**

Assigning Priority

An organization needs to be able to prioritize the activities it plans to work on. It needs to know which activities are most crucial to its success so that time and resources are not wasted on tactics that do not add value. Prioritization helps the organization determine who does what and when.

Accountability

Accountability means that an organization is clear on what needs to be measured in order to show success and who is accountable for that success. Employees need to know what results are expected of them so that they can align their actions with those expected results.

Harmony

When key pieces of the activities being performed are aligned to the same goal—the strategy the organization has laid out—that is harmony. Without that alignment, the organization will be moving in several directions at the same time. It's like an orchestra in which the musicians are each playing different music instead of the same piece.

Let's review the four numbered areas in the figure—where priority, accountability, and harmony overlap—to help you assess where you are.

1. Unclear Vision. Sometimes an organization is able to prioritize its activities and tactics and has established accountability within the organization for generating results, but there is no harmonization; in such a case, the direction of the organization is unclear. The activities being worked on and the accountabilities for success don't align with the organization's future vision. People are doing great work, but that work doesn't always generate results or add value to the organization.

2. Wasted Effort. When there are accountability for results and harmonization of the tactics and the future vision but no prioritization of those tactics, the efforts of employees are often wasted. They become engaged in busywork; everyone has the right intention, but they are working on the wrong activities. Important, value-generating activities are often forgotten as employees work on things that are easier and more comfortable. Without prioritization, the organization wastes time and resources on activities that add very little value, while the ones that can add value are ignored.

3. Poor Results. When there are prioritization and harmonization but no accountability, results are poor. Employees know what they need to do, and there is alignment with the future vision, but there is no accountability for results. Impacts can include duplication of effort or various activities not being done because employees are unsure about who should be performing them. It's impossible for an organization to thrive without accountability.

4. Execution Excellence. This occurs in the sweet spot where priority, accountability, and harmony all intersect. Organizations that fall into this category know what the most important activities are, they have ensured that those activities align with the future vision of the organization, and there is clear accountability for success. Organizations know what to measure to show success and who is accountable for success or failure.

Where would you plot yourself on this figure?

HOW TO ACHIEVE EXECUTION EXCELLENCE

Let's assume that we all want to become masters of execution so that we can get things done and done well. Organizations need to do several things to master that skill.

Have a Clear Strategy. This sounds so obvious I considered omitting it from this list, but it is really the starting point for the successful execution of any strategy. An organization needs to have a clear strategy that is easily understood and effectively communicated to internal staff and external stakeholders. "We want to grow by 12 percent in the northeastern United States in the next 12 months" is a much clearer strategy than "We are in growth mode." A strategy may not be completely right, or it may even be wrong, but it must always be easy to understand.

Develop an Execution Plan. An organization needs to have a plan for how the strategy will be achieved. This plan includes not only the central activities but also the key metrics and accountabilities. It outlines how the strategy will be accomplished (remember that strategy is the what, and the tactical execution is the how). This plan will encompass many of the elements to be discussed in this chapter and will provide a clear path for how the organization will accomplish its strategy.

Set Clear Expectations. It is important for an organization to set clear expectations for its employees, and those expectations should focus on results and outcomes. All employees should know exactly how they are going to contribute to driving the organization forward. Setting clear expectations for performance makes reviewing performance a much easier process.

Establish Appropriate Metrics. Because people often behave in a way that aligns with the way that they are being measured, you need to establish metrics that drive people toward your clearly stated strategy. This may mean changing the way your organization compensates its sales representatives or employees who work on the production line. If employees are clear on how their performance will be assessed and reviewed, they are more likely to behave in a way that aligns with those goals.

Review Performance Regularly. Although there is no right answer to the question of how often an organization should review the performance of its people, I do know that annually is not frequently enough. A lot can happen in a year; why wait that long to find out that someone is not performing up to expectations? It is management's job to constantly ensure that their teams are moving forward in a direction that aligns with the chosen strategy. In the next point, I suggest that organizations should review their strategy every three months. Why not review performance at the same time? Setting clear expectations and establishing metrics that align with them should make it fairly simple to determine who is performing well and who is not.

Constantly Review Your Strategy. An organization must constantly review its strategy to ensure that it still makes sense. I'm not talking about a full-blown strategy retreat and a detailed strategy development process; these should be considered relics anyway. I'm talking about a few smart people sitting around and asking, "Does this strategy still make sense? Will it still get us to where we want to be?" The marketplace is constantly changing, and sometimes organizations need to change with it. The only way to do that is to constantly review where you are going. Strategy is organic, and it needs to be assessed regularly.

Establish Accountability. Following the hypothetical case study presented next, I will discuss the difference between responsibility and accountability, but it's important to understand who is ultimately accountable for success. It's not going to be a team, a committee, or even something that's shared between two people. Ultimately, accountability falls on the shoulders of one person, and that accountability can't be assigned. Yet the most successful organizations flourish when their employees take on that accountability as their own.

An Example: Ace Enterprises

Let's take an example of a hypothetical company—we'll call it Ace Enterprises, a company that is looking to grow in the northeastern United States —to demonstrate how to apply these principles. Here is the company's path to execution excellence:

- ◆ Ace Enterprises has set a clear strategy that is easy to understand: "We want to grow by 12 percent in the northeastern United States in the next 12 months." That strategy is easy to communicate and easy to digest.

- ◆ Ace needs to develop an execution plan for how it will achieve its strategy. Let's assume that this growth will come from existing customers because the time and cost required for new customer acquisition are too great. The execution plan then needs to focus on retaining existing customers and how to sell them additional products and services. This approach should involve stratifying the existing customer base to focus on customers in the northeastern United States that have the greatest growth potential. Ace employees must focus most of their efforts in the areas that have the largest opportunity for growth.

♦ Ace now needs to set clear expectations for its employees. People in each of the key roles in the organization need to understand how they can contribute to meeting and even exceeding the strategic objective. Ace needs to establish clear expectations with its account and sales representatives about managing the existing customer base, and those expectations need to be focused on increasing retention and growing business with those existing accounts. Any employee who deals with a customer needs to identify new opportunities with that customer; employees going out on service calls may need to behave differently in order to generate leads. Every touch point with a customer becomes an opportunity for growth.

♦ Ace needs to then align its metrics with its goal of growing business with its existing customers. It needs to reward employees for gaining additional business with existing customers. Ace needs to look for areas of opportunity where it didn't look before. It could measure how many customer complaints are turned into new sales or how many service calls present additional opportunities.

♦ Since Ace employees now know exactly what is expected of them (expectations) and how their performance will be measured (clear metrics), managers within the organization need to constantly review employees' performance against those expectations and metrics. If an employee's performance is not satisfactory, then the managers need to determine whether it is a skills issue (the employee has not yet learned the right skills to be successful) or a capability issue (the employee is not motivated or capable of achieving the expected results). Managers can then take the appropriate steps to correct the poor performance (training or redeployment).

♦ Ace then needs to constantly review its strategy to ensure that it still makes sense, and management must have the ability to make changes. If the northeastern United States is suddenly hit with a stretch of terrible weather, Ace Enterprises may need to look in a different region for growth. If a competitor drops out of the market, then Ace Enterprises may see an opportunity to grow by acquiring new customers and thus may need to change its tactics. Ace Enterprises needs to be flexible in order to assess and act on new opportunities that may arise.

♦ Finally, Ace needs to identify who is responsible for the success or failure of the growth strategy. The best situation is when employees assume accountability for the strategy on their own but ultimately one person is accountable. Ace needs to determine who is ultimately on the hook for the success or failure of this strategy and to give that person the power to make decisions to make it happen.

THE DIFFERENCE BETWEEN RESPONSIBILITY AND ACCOUNTABILITY

In the context of business, we often talk about accountability and responsibility and use the terms interchangeably, but they are not the same. Responsibility means performing an action, whereas accountability means producing an outcome.

Think of a production line on which each worker has a different job. Workers are responsible for doing their jobs to the best of their ability, but they are not accountable for the success of the final product because they impact only a portion of the process that results in the final product.

Who is accountable for ensuring the final product that comes off the production line, ready to be delivered to a customer?

Generally, it would be someone who oversees the entire production line (like a plant manager or supervisor). We can't be expected to be accountable for something that we can't fully influence, can we?

How can we ensure accountability within an organization when we can't directly influence so many areas? We hear about many situations where leaders try to avoid accountability when their organizations make mistakes. And, in fact, accountability is truly achieved only when individuals hold themselves accountable. There is not much an organization can do to force people to be accountable for their areas of influence.

> **Responsibility has to do with performing an activity. Accountability relates to producing a result or outcome.**

Accountability is not about money, or job security, or status. True accountability comes from within each of us in the way we act, what we say, and how we treat others. It is about self-mastery and taking ownership for things we are involved with. Once we have mastered who we are and what we believe, we become accountable for those things we can control or those things that are ours to achieve. We are accountable because we have an emotional investment in the outcome, not because of positive reinforcement or the threat of negative consequences.

That is why accountability must ultimately fall on the shoulders of one person. A group of people can't have true accountability because in that case no one takes ownership for success or failure.

Tony Hayward of British Petroleum spent weeks blaming others for the oil spill his company caused in 2010, even though he was the one who was ultimately accountable. He was the CEO when his company's tanker leaked the oil. Yet he focused on what his suppliers and business partners did wrong. He took no accountability for the spill, even though it was his to take. At the time, he didn't seem worried that he might get fired, or go to jail, or become public enemy number one.

External forces don't influence whether we hold ourselves accountable for success and failure. It's fear that makes us avoid taking accountability, and it's a sense of ownership that draws us to it.

The most successful organizations hire people who hold themselves accountable for expected outcomes, regardless of the incentives or disincentives that may be in place. These are the companies that everyone wants to work for and be associated with.

Here are the three keys to having an organization built on accountability:

Create an Emotional Connection Between Your Customers and Your Employees. Ensure that your employees recognize the effect of putting out a low-quality product or service so that they are motivated to do better. Encourage them to own what gets put in front of your customers so that they will feel a sense of ownership to ensure that customers' expectations are exceeded.

Hire People Who Are Interested in Self-Development and Personal Growth. Such employees tend to take on more accountability for the outcomes they deliver because they recognize the value of taking responsibility for their own lives and looking for ways to improve. Their attitude is usually one of constant personal growth and searching for more effective ways to achieve better results, both personally and professionally. Someone who asks provocative questions is an example of someone interested in development and learning.

Provide Employees the Opportunity to Try Something and Fail. When something doesn't work out, you see employees' true colors and how resilient they are. Do they feel compelled to try again until they are successful, or do they focus on all the reasons it didn't work? Encouraging employees to try and fail creates a culture of innovation and growth and prevents organizational stagnation (when an organization's main focus is on what it has done in the past).

Creating a culture of accountability starts with the hiring decisions you make, so don't ignore that when determining the type of culture you want. When you hire inquisitive people who take ownership for their own lives, it's no coincidence that they will also take on ownership for the success of the organization they work for.

GAINING A TACTICAL ADVANTAGE: FINDING PERFORMANCE BOOSTS WHERE YOU WOULDN'T NORMALLY LOOK

The word *performance* can be used in many different ways. In this book, I have used it to describe the effectiveness with which a company operates. Performance and operational excellence go hand in hand, and better performance is often one of the outcomes achieved by a company that pursues operational excellence.

When an organization improves performance, results in other areas also improve. Profitability goes up. Retention of employees goes up. Customer loyalty goes up.

The challenge for many organizations is that often they don't look for potential performance boosts in what they already have. They generally look for cost savings or growth opportunities. If they do look for performance boosts, they tend to look in those same areas.

A true performance boost is when an organization finds a new opportunity, using existing resources that will have a material impact on its bottom line, and then exploits it. The best organizations are able to find performance boosts in areas where the competition doesn't normally look. Here are some places organizations normally look:

- Asking procurement to find cost savings from suppliers
- Reducing the number of employees
- Reducing the number of products or services the organization sells

- Reducing the professional development and training budgets
- Eliminating perks for certain employees
- Reducing employee travel
- Raising prices

There is nothing wrong with pursuing any or all of these areas to improve profitability, but many of these actions are focused on reduction, contraction, and cutting costs. If you focus only on cutting costs, you are not focused on growth and innovation. If you are not focused on growth and innovation, you will barely survive.

Consider this analogy. Those of you who travel by train or subway are probably familiar with the phrase "Mind the gap" or "Watch the gap." Between the subway or train car and the station platform, there is always a gap; signs everywhere warn people to be careful. You often see people drop things into the gap accidentally, trip over the gap, jump over the gap, and even little kids who are afraid to cross over the gap.

When approaching a gap, most organizations identify ways to prevent themselves from falling through the gap or tripping over it. They build bridges over the gap. They avoid the gap altogether. They try to make the gap smaller. But what if they tried to exploit the gap? What if they were able to turn that gap into a competitive advantage and a game-changing opportunity? Doing that would give the organization a performance boost in an area where most organizations don't typically look. That's what we're going to talk about in this section.

One of the great competitive advantages an organization can have is being able to find money and performance boosts in areas where most other organizations don't normally look. Here are 11 tactical areas where organizations can exploit gaps but where most organizations don't. All of these insights are discussed in more detail elsewhere in this book.

Obsess About Customer On-Boarding and Retention

Instead of focusing only on the *acquisition* of new customers, organizations should measure the seamless *on-boarding* of new customers and the *reten-*

If you look for opportunities in the same areas as everyone else, you achieve some improvements. If you look for opportunities where others don't, you create competitive advantage.

tion of existing customers. This is an opportunity that most organizations ignore. Once customers have decided to buy your products or services, you need to create a strong emotional connection with them in order to turn them into loyal customers.

Most organizations move on to the next potential sale and forget about the connection they've just made, thus losing the opportunity to exploit an opportunity that presents itself every time a new customer is acquired. Don't forget that a growing business has to spend more time and effort to acquire new customers than it does to keep existing customers.

Derive Revenue from Customer Complaints

Instead of focusing on resolving customer complaints, organizations should measure the amount of new revenue generated from those complaining customers. When a customer calls to complain about an issue, two key elements are present: The customers care enough about the product or service to take the time to call and complain; when they do make the call, they are a captive audience. Most customers just want their issue resolved quickly and to their satisfaction.

Consider how happy customers are when their issue has been resolved. Their level of stress has been reduced, and your organization was responsible for doing that. That is a great time to let them know about a product that will help avoid the same problem next time or a new service that would be of interest.

Turning those complaints into new sales is something most organizations rarely consider, but all it takes is a change in the way that service representatives deal with customers who call with a problem. Don't approach the situation merely as a necessary evil; see it also as an opportunity for growth.

My young daughter recently spilled water all over my laptop, and it shut down. I was anxious that I might lose all of the data and files. A tech store near my office was able to dry the circuit board and save not only all my data but my laptop as well. I was so grateful. After I left the store, it occurred to me that they had lost a great opportunity to sell me something. After almost losing all of my data, I would have considered buying an external storage device to back it up or even a service that backs up data for me, but no one ever asked me if I would like to hear more about those options.

Identify areas that you can exploit when customers have issues that need to be resolved or can be avoided.

Draw Customers to You

Instead of focusing only on pursuing new customers, find ways to have customers seek you out. Your organization needs to become an object of interest so that you can draw customers to you. People in the marketing world might call this "branding." When you have a strong brand, people are drawn to you. When people are drawn to you, the cost of new customer acquisition is reduced, and you are able to create loyal customers more quickly.

Social media, blogging, and the Internet make it easier than ever to get your ideas out there. If you understand what motivates your customers to buy, you can develop mechanisms to best attract them to you. It might be exclusive events, sharing valuable insights for free, hosting networking events, or even providing discounts.

Figure out what will bring your customers to you; then continue to offer them value so that they keep coming and bring others with them.

Measure Product Adoption

Instead of focusing only on product development timelines, measure the uptake of that product relative to other new products that were either successful or not.

Many organizations focus on the product development process and manage the time to market, but they don't focus enough on the uptake of that new product. It's a waste of time if you are able to get products to market quickly and effectively but no one buys them. It's an equal waste if you get good products to market slowly and ineffectively and are too late to take advantage of an opportunity.

Organizations should strike a balance between the speed and effectiveness of their product launches. You want to get to market as quickly and effectively as possible, with confidence that there is a strong market for your product. Measure the adoption of new products by customers and the time it takes so that you can find ways to improve the process and make it faster and more effective.

Don't Overdeliver

Instead of overdelivering on features, benefits, and services, determine what the customer needs and provide only that. I know this one sounds counterintuitive, but companies often provide functionality that customers don't need or don't have the time to learn. This is the danger of selling features and benefits instead of solutions that solve or enhance customer situations. Clayton Christensen, author of *The Innovator's Dilemma*, calls this *performance oversupply*. I call it a waste of time and resources.

If you understand the expectations of your customers, then you can easily exceed them. If you know what is important to them, then you can provide it. If you make wrong assumptions, you exhaust time and resources developing features and functionality that provide no value to your customers. Make sure you know what is valuable to your customers.

Focus on Successful Product Commercialization

Instead of measuring the number of new ideas you have developed, measure the number of ideas that have become commercially viable and determine where those ideas were generated. It's important to know how many ideas are being developed overall and where those ideas are coming from, but it's more important to know how many of those ideas are being turned into commercially viable products.

This opportunity for boosting performance is consistent with a theme throughout this book: Don't measure activities; instead, measure results and outcomes. If you focus only on the volume of ideas being generated, then you may do a good job of encouraging new ideas even though none of them benefit the organization.

We need to change the way we approach fostering innovation. We need to encourage new ideas but also encourage the ideas that make a difference. It's safe to say that most organizations don't track where some of their most successful ideas come from. If some of the best ideas come from customers or from a specific department in your organization, wouldn't you want to know that so that you could harness that power?

Measure the Rate of Customer Referrals

Instead of focusing on customer satisfaction, measure the number of referrals to new prospective customers provided by existing customers.

I'm always amazed at the importance organizations put on the concept of customer satisfaction. Just because customers complete a survey and say that they are satisfied doesn't mean the organization is going to be successful; it all depends on the questions being asked and the timing of those questions. High customer satisfaction scores mean only that an organization is meeting the expectations of its customers. This is a good thing, but what if those expectations are too low? Then the organization is losing a great opportunity to be even better.

A true indicator of customer satisfaction is the number of potential customers they have referred to your organization. Think about it. When you have found a doctor or dentist or contractor with whom you are happy and who has done a great job for you, you are more than happy to refer that person to your friends and family. Your customers are no different. If they believe others can derive value from what you offer, they want to be associated with that value, and they are more than happy to share their experiences and refer other people to you. This is the exponential value of customer retention, discussed in Chapter 6.

Stratify Your Customers

Instead of treating all customers equally, treat your most important customers better than the rest. It's a nice mantra to say that all customers are equal, but we know it's not true. You should be treating all customers well, but that doesn't mean that you treat them all the same way. You should be segmenting your customers based on specific criteria so that you treat your best customers better than the rest.

To do this, you need to treat each customer in a way that is consistent with how they expect to be treated. Customers who spend the most money with you and offer you the most referrals to other potential customers expect to be treated differently than other customers.

Determine the right criteria to stratify your customer base and to determine the appropriate behavior for each group of customers. You can even extend this stratification to your prospective customers to ensure that you are focusing business development efforts in the right place.

Determine an Acceptable Rate of Employee Turnover

Instead of measuring employee turnover or attrition, measure how many of your best people stay with the organization for more than three years. It's great to say that your organization has a low turnover rate because this implies that employees want to stay with the organization.

But what if the employees who are staying are actually the ones you wish would leave? There is an acceptable level of turnover within an organization because required skills change as organizational drivers change. Consider using a more targeted metric that focuses on the turnover among your best employees and those targeted for key roles within the organization.

It's important to be able to retain employees in the overall organization, but it's even more important to retain the ones who will be the future leaders of the organization and the ones who are the best performers. Compare your overall turnover rate to the turnover rate of your key employees. Which one is higher?

Reward Long-Term Customer Relationships

Instead of providing incentives to salespeople for making initial sales, measure and reward them only for repeat, long-term customers.

This goes against everything we have believed about sales since the beginning of time. We have always rewarded salespeople for making the initial sale and encouraged them to make more initial sales. However, we may be limiting the long-term potential with certain customers by focusing primarily on the first sale.

By mainly rewarding the first sale, we encourage sales representatives to close a deal and then move on to the next prospective customer. When we reward our reps for generating additional sales with the same customer, that customer becomes a more loyal customer, and the incentive for the rep is to build deeper, longer-term relationships. These longer-term relationships will increasingly benefit both your organization and your customers as the partnership strengthens.

Measure New Product Revenues Separately

Instead of focusing on the number of new products and services you bring to market, measure the percentage of revenue and profit those new products and services represent in their first three years of existence. I have clients who use this as the most important measurement within their organization because it indicates how well they innovate. But—and this is more important—it shows how well those innovations are being adopted in the marketplace. We typically look at time to market and the activities required to get to market. But what we should really be looking at is the uptake and adoption once the product or service enters the market. The better an organization becomes at accelerating this adoption and increasing the percentage of revenue from new products, the more innovative it will be and the faster it will grow.

PERFORMANCE BOOSTS: THE DO-IT-YOURSELF VERSION

One of the key competencies organizations need to learn is how to identify these areas of opportunity on their own. Feel free to tackle any or all of the ones I identified in the previous section, but if you want to master this skill on your own, here are some questions to consider:

- What areas of your organization have not been recently reviewed, updated, or changed (business processes, organizational structure, etc.)?
- How can you provide more value to customers in markets where there is a shifting business model?
- How are you attracting the right talent for your current and future needs?
- What kind of company do you want to be, and what do you need to do to achieve that?
- What areas of your organization have potential that has not yet been exploited?
- What is happening in your industry or with your competitors that you can gain from?

Finding performance boosts doesn't always have to come from something within your organization. Sometimes opportunities present themselves from the outside. Airbus has had a tremendous opportunity to capitalize on the challenges Boeing has had getting its Dreamliner airplane off the ground. Boeing's Dreamliner has experienced delay after delay in production; it finally made it through final approval, only to be grounded again with a mechanical issue. Unfortunately, Airbus has not been able to take advantage of this opportunity. But that's not because the opportunity wasn't there. It's because Airbus was not looking for opportunities in the right places and wasn't able to take advantage of the right opportunity when it presented itself.

A FINAL WORD ON STRATEGY EXECUTION

Strategy needs to be organic, and it needs to be constantly reviewed and updated based on customer behavior, competitors, legislation, and many other factors. Organizations should be reviewing strategies on a quarterly basis and quickly making the appropriate updates.

The area where most organizations need to focus more effort is on the execution of the strategy. How are you going to achieve your strategy successfully? What tactics need to be employed? What metrics will you use to show success?

Don't develop strategy in an offsite retreat or only in the C-suite offices; instead, consider including employees from all levels of the organization. Execution is smoother and more successful when the people who must execute the strategy have been involved in its formulation. There are examples throughout this book of companies with great strategies but poor execution; it's the poor execution that leads to poor results.

CHAPTER 6

ACQUIRING AND KEEPING THE CUSTOMERS YOU WANT

THIS CHAPTER IS BUILT ON two key principals, and neither of them is, "The customer is always right." The key principles are that your current customers represent your best opportunity for profitable growth and that most organizations know this but don't do much about it.

How many organizations do you know that ask for referrals from their customers? It's not as many as you think. I'd say it's about 25 percent.

How many of those organizations then follow up effectively on those referrals? Probably no more than half of that 25 percent.

Now, how many of those organizations actually measure the number of referrals they receive from their customers or the amount of business that comes from those referrals?

Very few, say 10 percent.

What can we conclude? Assuming my math is correct, that means that only 1 percent or 2 percent of all organizations are actually asking for, following up on, and measuring the business they receive from referrals from existing customers.

And you thought it was difficult to differentiate yourself and grow profitably? Look no further.

The easiest and quickest way to grow your customer base is through referrals from existing customers.

A quick aside: The potential for customer referrals is an excellent example of an untapped opportunity as organizations search for ways to grow profitably and quickly.

WHY CURRENT CUSTOMERS ARE YOUR BEST OPPORTUNITY FOR GROWTH

The hardest business to get is from a new customer. You must cultivate the relationship, show the value of your product or service, prove your credibility, and then ask a customer to part with their money. As most of us know, it's not easy asking people to part with their money.

So it would be a logical conclusion that it is much easier to generate business from existing customers than to acquire new ones. Why don't all organizations focus more on customer retention and leveraging their existing customer relationships? I don't know, but failing to exploit this opportunity is a mistake.

Let's take the example of one customer and the potential value he or she represents for your organization:

1. A customer buys an initial product from you.

2. The customer then buys that same initial product more frequently.

3. The customer then buys additional, higher-margin products from you.

4. The customer then tells his or her friends and colleagues

about your organization and refers other customers to your products or services.

5. The new customers then buy an initial product or service from you, thus potentially taking business away from your competition and reducing your customer acquisition costs.

6. The cycle begins with those new customers.

The end result is that you grow your business, your market share increases, and you price your products higher, so your profitability increases. You also create a cycle of constant growth through customer retention. These dramatic results stem from focusing on the retention of one customer. Do you see the value in that?

If not, maybe Figure 6-1 will help. It shows how making the initial sale with one customer can lead to outward expansion with not only that one customer but also with the people in his or her network.

Some of you might remember a television commercial from the 1980s with Heather Locklear (if not, you can find it on YouTube). In this commercial, Locklear tells us about the first time she used Faberge Organic shampoo, "It was so good that I told two friends about it, and they told two friends, and so on, and so on, and so on." That is the exponential value of customer retention. And you don't need to be Heather Locklear to take advantage of it.

If you do a good job of retaining customers, they can become evangelists and ambassadors for your brand. Nothing increases your credibility more than having your customers speak highly of your products and services without being prompted to do so. It saves you a whole lot of time and money. Throughout this chapter, I will provide you with various strategies to improve customer retention and leverage the exponential value of your customers.

Meanwhile, let's look at an example of a company that has expanded its reach exponentially. Lululemon Athletica, a Canadian company, makes yoga pants and other athletic clothing for men

Figure 6-1. The Exponential Value of Customer Retention

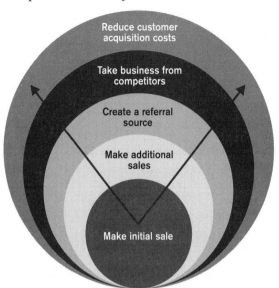

and women. The amazing thing about Lululemon's products is not just that they make everyone look great and feel good about themselves but that Lululemon has created an entire community around its products. It has become a symbol for a certain lifestyle—eating healthy, exercising, protecting the environment. The Lululemon brand is not just about a pair of comfortable yoga pants.

Lululemon has tapped into a group of like-minded customers who have been brought together through the products and the philosophy of the organization. The company has established a strong emotional connection with their customers (see the following section) through their corporate philosophy and grassroots initiatives. Lululemon is very active in local communities, promoting a healthy lifestyle and environmental protection.

It has partnered with local organizations to push that lifestyle out to everyone and has created many ambassadors along the way. Those ambassadors might be employees or customers or yoga instructors or local governments or fitness centers; they all believe in the Lululemon corporate philosophy and want to make a positive impact on their communities.

How to Leverage the Exponential Value of Customer Retention for Profitable Growth

To become an expert in customer retention, a key tool for profitably growing your business, you must learn to leverage your existing customers. Retention is more than just customer satisfaction. Customers may be satisfied, but that doesn't mean they will buy from you again or tell everyone they know about you.

Here are seven ways to improve customer retention so that you can leverage the exponential value of your current customers.

1. Create a Strong Bond with the Customer as Quickly as Possible. Once a customer has purchased something from you, make the initial experience a positive one. Give her an incentive to buy more, make the on-boarding process easy, or give her a call to thank her for her business. Don't waste this great opportunity to create loyalty from the outset.

2. Make the Customer Feel as Though He or She Is Your Only Customer. Customers don't care that you are having a bad day or that you have been frustrated by another customer. Don't rush them off the phone. Don't ignore their e-mails. Provide them with the support they need, regardless of other issues that might need resolving.

3. Recognize That All Customers Are Not Equal. The stratification of customers is very important, and I will cover this in more detail in the next section. Some customers should be contacted monthly; others can be contacted annually. You should not treat your best customers the same as your worst customers. Identify the key criteria to determine your best customers (potential growth, history of purchases, level of influence, length of service, and so on). Develop different customer tiers, and treat each tier accordingly.

4. Proactively Communicate with Customers, Not Just When You Have Something to Sell Them. Customers know when you are trying to sell them something and will stop responding if they think that is the only reason you call or contact them. Provide them added-value special reports, exclusive previews, or special discounts on what they currently buy to ensure that they will always take your call.

5. Give Them the Opportunity to Be Involved. Some of your customers want to be involved by sitting on a product development panel or providing feedback on your newest commercials. Giving your best customers the opportunity to participate will pull them closer to your brand.

6. Be Open and Transparent in Your Communications. Never lie. Customers know when you are not telling the truth, which is one of the quickest ways to lose their loyalty. Even when you have bad news to share, share it openly and communicate what you are doing to resolve the issue and to ensure it never happens again. Customers can be very forgiving when they are treated with respect and integrity.

7. Manage Expectations. Do what you say you are going to do, and let customers know if anything changes. Be sure that you meet or exceed expectations. When you are late with a product launch or when features of a service are not what was promised, your reputation will suffer.

Customer retention is one of the most important ways to grow your business. Current customers represent the easiest market to target for additional growth. They are already familiar with your company and what you offer, so why not focus on them? Too many organizations think they need only new customers to grow, but that is not the case. Depending on the size of your organization, identify your 10 or 100 or 1,000 best customers, and do something special for them. It won't take long to see great results.

STRATIFYING YOUR CUSTOMERS

To *stratify* is to arrange things into groups or classes. How does this apply to customers? Very simply: You need to arrange your customers into groups. It's up to you to decide on the criteria you will use to arrange them, but regardless of the number of customers you have, you should deal with them differently. The old adage that "All customers are equal" is simply not true. All customers deserve to be treated well, but you should not treat them all the same way.

Why It's Important to Treat Customers Differently

As a consumer, have you ever been somewhere and felt you were being treated differently than other customers? You arrive at a hotel and someone else gets priority check-in before you. You are waiting in the security line at the airport and the frequent fliers jump in front of you. You wait 45 minutes to get a table at a new restaurant, and a couple who just arrived gets seated before you.

This is the stratification of customers in action. Every organization does it, consciously or unconsciously. I'm here to tell you that you should be doing it—consciously.

And I'll let you in on a little secret: The best organizations in the world stratify their customers, but none of their customers feel as though they are being treated poorly. And even if those customers are being treated differently, the best organizations treat all of their customers as if they are the only customer.

All customers are not created equal. Treat all customers as though they are your only customer, but treat different customers in different ways.

I was recently in Las Vegas at the Wynn Hotel. This beautiful property hosts thousands of customers at any given time, but it does not treat all of them the same way. The hotel has a main registration desk for hotel guests who pay regular rates for regular rooms and a separate entrance for guests staying in the suites and villas. The customers in the second group are obviously paying the hotel more money and expect a different level of service. And they get it—concierge service for anything they need, a private entrance and check-in desk, access to additional amenities, and many other perks.

But the other customers never feel slighted that some customers are treated differently because everyone is treated well. People are disappointed only if they are not treated with the level of service they think they deserve. (Let's ignore the small percentage of customers who feel entitled to the best service while paying the lowest rate.)

The key to employing a successful customer stratification strategy is *to provide a level of service and support that corresponds with the level of purchase the customer is making.* Each organization will determine that appropriate level of support and service, and some will even provide too much. But it is a balanced approach that makes an organization successful.

Criteria for Determining Your Most Important Customers

Take a look at Figure 6-2 for a very simple example of stratifying customers. You can use any criteria you like in making this determination; here are a few:

- Amount of money spent with your organization
- Frequency of purchases
- Number of referrals provided
- Growth potential
- Social influence
- Length of time as a customer

Four Key Groups of Customers

Figure 6-2 divides your customers into four groups, with the best customers in the bull's-eye in the middle of the target.

Figure 6-2. Customer Stratification

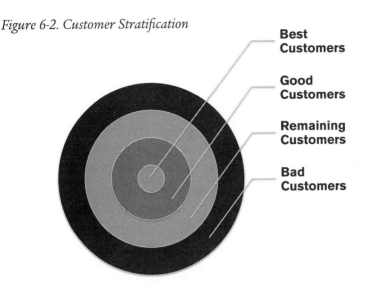

Best Customers. You want to take the most time getting to know and engaging these customers, who typically represent only 5–10 percent of your customer base but may account for as much as 40–50 percent of your revenue. You want to offer these customers unique experiences and provide them with something other customers are not privy to. These customers can be great sources of referrals to new potential customers and thus a great source of growth for your organization.

Good Customers. These customers typically represent 15–20 percent of your customer base and about the same amount of your revenue base. They have probably been loyal customers for a few years, but they will never make the jump to being the best ones. You need to engage them in unique ways to ensure they stay with you and even bring new potential customers to you.

Remaining Customers. This group represents the largest number of customers, perhaps even upward of 80 percent, but they represent only 20–30 percent of your revenue. You want to continue to engage with these customers who form such a high proportion of your customer base; do so in ways that don't require too much time and effort but that still make these customers feel special.

Bad Customers. These are customers who actually cost you money. Earlier I alluded to a small group of customers who feel entitled to receive better service and support than they deserve; those are the bad customers. They constantly ask for better service while wanting to pay less. They drain your resources and take time away from your best customers. Later in this chapter, I will discuss when and how to fire these bad customers.

How to Treat Each Level of Customers to Make Them Feel Special

There are ways to engage each of the top three levels of customers to ensure that you are providing service and support corresponding to the purchasing by those customers and their value to your organization.

The key to being successful is knowing how to treat each customer group so that all your customers feel satisfied with the level of service and support they are receiving. The only way to know that is to determine your customers' expectations and exceed them.

Most customers acknowledge that they need to pay more or buy more to get an increased level of support. Yet those customers still have expectations. They still expect to be treated with respect. They still expect their issues to be resolved quickly. They may expect a courtesy phone call every so often. It is imperative that you know what each of your customer groups expects so you can deliver it to them.

Let's take the example of a bank. Banks have many different types of customers—personal banking, commercial banking, corporate banking, investors, and so on. Those customers who have only a savings account with a bank don't expect the same level of treatment as someone with a million-dollar portfolio with that same bank. However, customers with a savings account still expect at least enough service to meet their needs. Courteous and efficient tellers, short wait times, access to their money whenever they need it, and assurance that their money will never be lost—these are only a few of their needs. If you can provide those and even provide some additional value, you will have loyal customers.

The customer with the million-dollar portfolio also has expectations on how he or she should be treated; those expectations might include monthly meetings, regular portfolio reviews, and other kinds of special treatment. The point is that understanding your customers' expectations goes a long way in effectively stratifying your customer base.

When to Fire Customers

Some customers are just not worth the effort. I'm sorry to say that out loud, but it's true. The key is determining who those customers are and finding the right way to fire them. Here are some reasons you might want to let some customers go:

- They are not profitable.
- They are not aligned with your future vision of success.
- They use up a great deal of resources and take time away from other customers.
- They expect a level of service that is not commensurate with the amount of business they provide.
- They are constantly trying to get additional products and services without making an additional investment.
- They are not your ideal target customer.

This situation is not like Donald Trump on *The Apprentice*. You do not have a meeting with your customer and say, "You're fired." There are more respectful and appropriate ways to let customers go when they no longer fit with the direction you want to go. Here are a few suggestions:

- Don't contact them. Get over the need to chase down every lead; don't contact those customer and prospective customers who you feel are not aligned with your future success. Most of them will leave through attrition.

- Suggest other alternatives. As your organization moves in a different direction, suggest other products, services, or even organizations that would be a better fit for what they need. In this case, sending a customer to one of your competitors might be a good thing.

- Shift your approach. You may decide to target a different set of customers; if so, at the same time, change your approach so that your organization no longer appeals to some of the customers you no longer want to do business with.

It is always a difficult decision to let customers go because no one likes to leave money on the table, but, as I **Sometimes you need to shed old customers in order to reach out to new ones.** once told a client, "How many opportunities are you losing by focusing your efforts on the wrong customers?"

HOW TO TURN CUSTOMERS INTO GREAT REFERRAL SOURCES

If you want to turn your customers into great referral sources, you need to do only two things: Provide constant value and ask them. If you have done a great job of providing value to customers, they will be more than happy to refer you to other potential customers. They will even be proud to do so because it makes them look good. All you need to do is ask.

What does it mean to constantly provide value? Here are some examples:

- You constantly provide a high-quality product or service.

- You provide customers with access to insights or information they can't get anywhere else.
- You make it easy for customers to do business with you.
- You resolve customer service issues rapidly and effectively.
- You invite customers to unique, exclusive events.
- You openly share information about your organization.
- You provide ways to make the lives of your customers better.
- You take an active role in making your community a better place.

If you do even some of these things, customers will want to be associated with you because they value the relationship, and they will be happy to tell others about you.

When it comes to asking for referrals, let's not make a bigger deal than it needs to be. It is actually quite simple. Here are a few phrases you can use:

- "We are always looking to grow our business, so please tell us if you know of someone who can benefit, as you did, from what we offer."
- "We gladly accept referrals to friends and family and very much appreciate those introductions. Do you know anyone who might be interested in what we offer?"
- "I see that you are very satisfied with our products. Do you know of others who might also enjoy them?"

We are all different, and we all have different ways of asking for referrals. The most important point is to just do it. *This is the single quickest way to grow your business quickly and profitably.*

When I first started my consulting business, I was fortunate enough to work with a client who was very well connected. We did some great work together for his organization, and I eventually asked if he would mind introducing me to some of his colleagues. I knew that he was quite influential within a particular group that contained members of ten other organizations. I asked whether he could introduce me to his peers in those organizations. He told me I could use his name when reaching out to them, so, of course, I did. As a result, I was able to meet with almost all of the ten organizations. This led to many great meetings and two new clients, one of which became one of my best. All I had to do was provide great value and ask.

Sometimes you will need to exert some effort to find the best method for asking for and receiving referrals. Some customers will do it quickly and easily, and others will need more support. And, of course, some customers will just never be good at giving you referrals, and that's OK because they are still great customers.

You need to know your customers and find the best approach to ask for and gather referrals from them. You also need to determine the right time to ask. Here are some of the right times:

- When you have a trusting relationship with the customer who understands your value.

- When you have a new product or service to offer.

- When you have recently resolved an issue for the customer or provided additional value.

- When customers tell you how satisfied they are with your products or services—in other words, when they provide a testimonial about the benefits of working with you.

I kept asking one of my best clients for referrals, and he was more than willing to provide them. He would always tell me that he would keep me in mind when talking to colleagues, but that failed to result in any introductions. I needed to make it easier for him to provide referrals, so I tried a different approach. The next time I asked for referrals, I had done some research and provided him with the names of three people whom I thought he might know and whom I wanted to meet. I then asked if he could introduce me to them. He was more than happy to do it, and that led to more great meetings and two new clients. Needless to say, I continue to use this strategy.

OTHER STRATEGIES TO STRENGTHEN CUSTOMER LOYALTY AND ENGAGEMENT

In this section, I will identify areas where you can strengthen customer loyalty and improve customer engagement. Hopefully, one or more of these strategies will align well with the strengths of your organization and the direction you want to go.

Customer On-Boarding

Picture this: You have just spent the last few weeks winning over a new prospective customer, and just yesterday she agreed to sign on to buy your product or service. Now what? If you are like most organizations, you will celebrate the success of acquiring another customer, you will enter her into your customer relationship management system, you will send her a bunch of forms to complete, and then you will forget about her and move onto the next opportunity.

Does this scenario sound familiar? If it does, you may be routinely wasting great opportunities to build loyal customers.

You have just put a great deal of effort into acquiring this new customer, so why would you ignore the opportunity to make her a great customer from the outset? By creating a positive experience in the on-boarding process, as I call it, where most other organizations falter, you will quickly create an ambassador for your company.

Most organizations don't recognize the value of accelerating the process of bringing on new customers once they have been acquired. This seems odd because clear benefits can be achieved by bringing on new customers more rapidly and more effectively:

- You speed up the process of gaining additional business from them.

♦ You receive referrals to other prospective customers sooner.

♦ You strengthen the relationship and increase customer loyalty and the likelihood of retention and growth.

♦ You use your own resources more effectively.

A company that I worked for a few years ago was awarded business from a new customer. The process of bringing the new customer on became so time-consuming and arduous that the customer walked away and instead went with our competitor. We asked him to provide the same information multiple times, we did not have an assigned support resource to help him through the process, and once he agreed to buy from us, we moved on to the next prospective customer without even trying to cultivate the new relationship. We lost not only the original business but also the opportunity to grow with that customer and turn him into a great business partner.

There is a tremendous opportunity in looking at the way you bring on new customers, but many organizations don't even consider this opportunity. And if they do, they don't know where to start. Figure 6-3 is an example of a customer on-boarding process developed with one of my clients (some details removed or changed for confidentiality).

We implemented this process for each new customer the client brought on in order to ensure that he took advantage of the opportunity to create a strong bond from the outset of the relationship. You will need to adjust this process depending on the goods or service that you provide, but be sure that you are able to complete all of the steps quickly and effectively.

Companies like iContact and Constant Contact make it very easy for their small business customers to begin using their e-mail marketing services. They provide easy-to-use templates, online support tools, and setup wizards to walk you through the initial setup process, and they have customer support staff available through phone and e-mail to address any questions customers may have.

Figure 6-3. A Customer On-Boarding Process

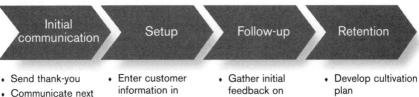

Initial communication	Setup	Follow-up	Retention
◆ Send thank-you ◆ Communicate next steps ◆ Identify key customer contacts ◆ Assign customer support resources ◆ Identify decisions that customer need to make	◆ Enter customer information in database ◆ Provide customer with product or service details ◆ Establish success metrics ◆ Determine other activities required	◆ Gather initial feedback on customer satisfaction ◆ Make appropriate changes based on initial feedback ◆ Identify anything else the customer needs	◆ Develop cultivation plan ◆ Engage customer in product/service planning ◆ Measure success and make appropriate changes

Are you making it easy for new customers to buy from you?

As you look for ways to improve and accelerate your on-boarding process, ask yourself these questions:

◆ What activities are we asking customers to perform that we could be doing for them?

◆ What activities are we asking them to perform that do not add measurable value to the process?

◆ What data can be gathered in advance of the customer being acquired that will accelerate the on-boarding process?

◆ What activities can be simplified or standardized (form completion, setup, and so on)?

◆ How can we use technology to automate activities that are being performed manually (such as form submission or data entry)?

◆ What decisions do customers need to make, and how can we help making those decisions easy for them?

◆ What support will customers require?

◆ How can we measure the process results so that we can improve performance in the future?

Once a customer agrees to buy your products and services, you have a great opportunity to create a strong bond right away. Don't ignore the importance of creating this loyalty early on. This will be the first experience a customer has with you. Take advantage of this opportunity to make a great first impression and to create a loyal customer for life.

What Do We Mean by the "Customer Experience"?

The best example of providing a positive customer experience happens at Disney theme parks around the world. When you arrive at a Disney park, you truly feel that you have entered a different world.

Here are a few of the things Disney does to create that unique experience:

♦ If you are staying at a Disney hotel, when you enter the property you check in first at the security booth. When you arrive at the front door of the hotel, they are expecting you and call you by name.

♦ The first person to greet you says, "Welcome home."

♦ You are checked into your room before even entering the front lobby of the hotel. A concierge greets you in front of the hotel with an iPad and gets you all settled in. You are checked in while they unload the luggage from the car.

♦ Every employee smiles at you and wishes you a "magical day."

♦ Every employee is empowered to make decisions in the best interest of the customer; that might mean replacing a dropped popcorn container or letting you go through a secret entry to go on a ride again.

♦ Each day, for guests of the Disney resorts, one of the theme parks opens an hour early or stays open an hour late.

♦ The theme parks regularly open five minutes before the official opening time.

You may think this all sounds corny, but you can't argue with this fact: 70 percent of all visitors to Disney theme parks come back at least once. That is a staggering level of customer retention. Can you say that about your customer retention strategies?

Dealing with Customer Complaints

In Chapter 5, I provided you with numerous areas where you can look for performance boosts that are often ignored. Dealing with customer complaints is one of those areas. Most organizations I deal with look at complaining customers as a necessary evil. They try to resolve problems as quickly as possible without being concerned about whether the issue was resolved appropriately or to the satisfaction of the customer.

What these organizations fail to realize is that when customers take the time to complain, they care about the resolution. And when this kind of emotion is involved, there is a great opportunity to create a loyal customer. Earlier in this chapter, I mentioned that one of the seven strategies to improve customer retention was to create a strong emotional bond. Well, here's your chance. These customers are already emotional because they are complaining. You need to harness that emotion and turn them into loyal customers.

How can you do that? It's simple. Resolve the issue quickly and effectively. Don't make customers jump through hoops or speak to multiple departments to get the issue resolved. Give them an opportunity to give the details of their complaint and take immediate steps to address it.

You will be amazed at the lengths customers are willing to go when they feel that someone has heard their concern and is addressing it. They become your biggest fan because you have just removed a stress from their life.

Providing Additional Value

The reason most customers don't answer the phone when you call is because they know why you're calling; to sell them something. Too often we call on our customers only when we want something from them. But what if we started calling them to offer them something? And I don't just mean a discount on your products and services. I mean something that would be of value to them.

I offer my clients and prospects a free monthly newsletter that is filled with articles, podcasts, and other information that I think will be valuable for them. Occasionally I offer a special report or exclusive information created specifically for my list. Here are some ideas for additional value you can offer your customers:

- Industry data they can't find elsewhere.
- Introductions to other customers for networking and collaboration opportunities.
- Referrals to new potential customers for their own business.
- Referrals to other organizations that would be of benefit.
- Access to exclusive events or experiences.

When you offer these kinds of additional value to your customers, not only will you get credit for helping them improve; you will also find that they will take your calls more often and even start telling people about what a great organization you are. This can only lead to more prospective customers.

THE FIVE MYTHS OF CUSTOMER ENGAGEMENT

Engaging customers in various ways is not a new concept in the business world, but organizations are now realizing how important this engagement can be. As with any strategy, myths have arisen about customer engagement—and I am here to debunk them.

Myth 1: Engaging Customers Means Asking Them What They Want

No. Engaging customers means getting them involved. It means giving them an exclusive preview or access to a product before the general public sees it or asking them to participate in new product development. However, it is not truly engagement when you simply ask customers what they want through an online survey or focus group. Yes, you are getting them involved, but being part of a focus group or completing an online survey does not create loyalty. Instead, imagine taking these steps with your customers:

- You call customers and tell them you would like their input on the next generation of a product you are developing.
- You invite them to join a customer panel and describe your new product to them.
- You ask them for feedback and insights.
- You follow up on their suggestions and let them know how you have handled each suggestion.
- You give them a sneak preview of the product before its official public launch.
- You invite them to a private, exclusive event to launch the new product.
- You publicly communicate that the customer was instrumental in helping you develop some of the features of this new product.

Which customers do you think will be loyal and more likely to refer you to new customers—the ones who you took through some or all of the preceding seven steps or those you simply contacted with an online survey?

Myth 2: Customers Will Tell Others About Your Company Just Because You Are Excellent

This is simply not true. Customers will tell others about you only if you provide a unique experience that is worth telling people about. Here are some examples:

- BMW dealers give every new potential customer the royal treatment. Friendly service, no pressure to buy, aesthetically pleasing environment, and association with a great brand. The dealers differentiate the BMW experience from what other car dealers provide.

- Apple stores are bright, open, and aesthetically pleasing; they allow customers to try new products and are staffed with knowledgeable people who can answer technical questions. They offer tutorials, workshops, data transfers, and live service people (the genius bar). Compare that to what Dell or Compaq or Lenovo or Samsung offer their customers as an experience.

- Porter Airlines offers fast check-in, a convenient downtown Toronto location, shuttle service, first-class lounge areas, and other perks that are included in the fare price. Compare those services to other airlines that charge extra for bags, snacks, advanced seat selection, and access to lounges, and you can see why many Canadian travelers choose Porter over Air Canada or WestJet.

Making quality products is certainly the first step in engaging customers because, without quality, your brand reputation will be poor. However, you need to provide more than just quality. You need to provide and continue to provide a memorable experience for your customers. Service is what keeps customers coming back and what prompts them to refer others.

What value are you providing your customers? When you create an emotional connection, your customers will feel that they are invested in your success and will do whatever they can to ensure that your success continues.

Myth 3: All Customers Are Equal

We all know that is not true, yet we continue to say it. Do you treat your ten best customers the same way you treat someone who has just walked in off the street? If so, you may be struggling to retain your best customers.

I have been a customer of Rogers Wireless for about ten years. My family has three cell phones with them, as well as numerous other products and services; like other families, mine will surely use an increasing number of wireless products and services as time goes on. When I recently tried to upgrade my phone, I learned that a new customer could receive a better deal than I could. I have spent close to $50,000 with this company, yet a new customer gets a better deal than I do. Does that make sense?

All customers are not created equal. However, the best companies have learned how to treat every customer as though they are their best. That doesn't mean you treat all customers the same way; it just means that you make every customer feel special.

You should be spending the most time and effort on your best customers and working on engaging and retaining them. You need to stratify your customers (see "Stratifying Your Customers" earlier in this chapter). You need to know which customers spend the most with you, which are most profitable, and which customers have the best potential to provide the exponential value of customer retention.

That doesn't mean you ignore the rest because you never know which new customers might eventually become your best ones. However, it does mean you focus on retaining and cultivating those who have proved to be loyal and profitable in the past.

Myth 4: Offering Customers Discounts Creates Customer Loyalty

Very few organizations have ever been successful by simply cutting costs. Cutting costs puts you in survival mode. I'm not suggesting that you never use discounts, but when you discount your price, you needlessly commoditize the products and services. The one-time savings opportunity makes every product and service offered a commodity: It's being sold based on lowest cost, not on any other factor.

A great example of this is Groupon, the company that offers its expansive customer base large discounts through daily deals. Groupon works with retailers, restaurants, local businesses, and other organizations and aggregates special offerings for customers. Groupon then takes a percentage of the price paid by the customer.

The problem with this model is that it is not sustainable and doesn't create customer loyalty for the participating organizations. Customers buy the discounted products or services through Groupon and then never return to the store or restaurant again. The purchase is motivated by cost savings, not by brand loyalty or an emotional connection. Organizations would be more successful if they provided a longer-term offer that would bring the customer back to them multiple times or somehow established an emotional connection and relationship with those customers.

Myth 5: Customer Engagement Is the Same as Customer Retention

The term *customer engagement* has been around a long time; it means different things to different organizations. To me, customer engagement is providing customers with unique experiences and with access that allow them to have a stake in the success of the organization. Apple gives certain bloggers access to products before they are launched to the public. Dell holds customer forums, bringing many of their corporate customers together to share knowledge and information. Indigo Books and Music allows customers to make suggestions on product improvement and store layout. These are all different ways to engage customers.

However, engaging customers is not the same as retention. Customer engagement can be used as a way to retain customers, but engaging customers doesn't make them loyal.

Engagement can be a part of the seven strategies for improving customer retention (discussed earlier in this chapter), but engagement itself does not automatically lead to retention.

With these five myths of customer engagement debunked, let me leave you with four key points to remember as you plan how to leverage the exponential value of customers:

1. Stratify your customers, and develop retention strategies for each customer level.

2. Current customers represent your best opportunity for profitable growth.

3. Provide a degree of service and support that corresponds with the investment each customer is making.

4. Develop strength in areas like customer on-boarding and fielding customer complaints to generate new revenue opportunities.

Building customer strategies based on these key points will provide your organization with a major thrust forward toward success.

CHAPTER 7

OPTIMIZING SPEED MAXIMIZES PROFITABILITY

WE OFTEN DON'T ASSOCIATE OPTIMIZING speed with impacting profitability. More often than not, organizations just focus on doing things faster. There are a time and a place for moving faster, but the best organizations know when to move faster, when to slow down, and when to maintain their speed. This chapter introduces the concept of *optimal enterprise velocity* and demonstrates why it's important to manage the speed at which your organization does business in order to maximize profitability and performance.

DETERMINING OPTIMAL ENTERPRISE VELOCITY AND RESPONSIBLE SPEED

You may have heard the phrase, "Stop and smell the roses." This phrase is a good way to describe what many organizations need to do. Too many organizations think that speed is only about moving faster, but the best organizations focus on managing speed optimization. They determine when it is best to speed things up and when it is best to slow things down. Sometimes it makes sense to actually slow down, take a look around, and then continue moving forward. The slowdown lets you see what is going on around you and make necessary adjustments.

Optimal enterprise velocity is the rate at which an organization does business without sacrificing the quality of its offerings—essentially, how fast an organization can move and still be effective. Knowing when to slow down and when to speed up, as well as having the ability to accelerate and brake accordingly, can change the success of a company overnight.

Think of your organization as a train. The track you follow is the strategy you have developed, the direction you have decided to pursue. The train stations are the milestones along the way toward your final destination; they represent the successful achievement of your objectives for the organization. Signals along the way tell a train conductor to speed up because another train is catching up or to slow down because other trains are ahead. In the same way, organizations should use their performance metrics as signals that allow management to set an optimal speed for the organization. What are the signals your organization uses to know when to speed up and when to slow down?

Look at the different areas of your business—product commercialization, strategy development, customer acquisition, employee hiring, and any others that are important for your organization—and ask yourself whether you have achieved optimal speed.

How will you know? What process should you go through to determine that speed?

Organizations that use their metrics as signals for governing their pace can achieve what I call *responsible speed*.

Accelerating results does not always mean moving faster. Assessing and acting on business opportunities require flexibility in operations and accountability in decision making. Businesses need to apply the principle of responsible speed to find out the speed they are most comfortable with—the speed that will allow them to achieve flourishing results.

I take some of my clients through a process to determine the optimal speed for their organizations. Here are the questions we begin with for each of their key areas:

- How fast are you going now?
- How fast could you go (what is your potential top speed)?
- What would happen if you were to achieve that top speed?
- What are the key indicators you should use to determine when to slow down and when to speed up?
- What plan do you need to put in place to maintain optimal speed?

We often use the wrong indicators to measure performance because we focus on simply going faster rather than on wisely governing speed. We measure customer service representatives on how fast they complete phone calls, not whether the customer's issue was resolved. We measure the speed of bringing a product to market without considering whether that product is any good or anyone will buy it. We measure the time it takes to hire new employees even though we have been experiencing high employee turnover rates. We measure the time it takes to process a purchase order but not whether the information included in the order is correct.

Instead of focusing on moving faster, organizations should manage their speed. Sometimes going too fast will hurt the organization, just as, at other times, going too slowly will **Sometimes you need to slow down in order to accelerate results.** impact performance. The most successful organizations are those that are able to move at their optimal speed at all times, recognizing that the organization's optimal speed changes depending on the situation.

Calibrating the speed at which an organization operates has

many advantages. Here are just a few reasons why you need to find your optimal enterprise velocity:

- ◆ You get new products and services to market faster by focusing on the ones that have the best commercial viability.
- ◆ You increase the effectiveness of your employees and allow them to work on more value-added activities or improve their life balance by leaving the office earlier or not working weekends.
- ◆ You attract strong, dynamic talent when you take the time to develop the right hiring and retention processes.
- ◆ You resolve customer service issues quickly and effectively.
- ◆ You increase the value of your relationships by taking the time to build stronger partnerships with suppliers and other business partners.
- ◆ You realize additional growth by building strong brand loyalty and taking the time to engage customers effectively.
- ◆ You make better decisions by knowing when to move quickly and when to gain further support.
- ◆ You acquire new customers with high growth potential because you focus on the best opportunities.

All these benefits have a direct or indirect positive impact on your company's bottom line, so why wouldn't you try to better manage the speed at which you operate?

Figure 7-1 shows how speed impacts performance. In this figure, a *relic* is an organization that doesn't manage speed and has poor performance. This organization doesn't recognize the value of managing speed and usually just tries to move faster and, in the process, more often than not sacrifices the quality of its offerings.

A *fad* doesn't manage its speed yet still has good performance, which usually occurs because of luck or past successes. The strong performance of this organization is not sustainable.

Figure 7-1. How Speed Impacts Performance

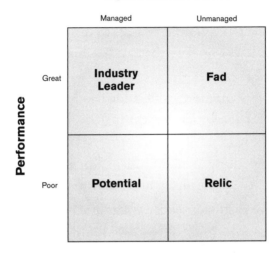

A *potential* is an organization that recognizes the value of managing speed but doesn't do it effectively. It rushes through decisions that require more time and slows down other processes when going faster would be advantageous. This organization doesn't know how to calibrate its speed.

An *industry leader* knows that the value of managing speed results in strong performance. Later in this chapter is a roadmap for becoming an industry leader. If you are already there, congratulations; there is something for you as well later.

Based on these descriptions, which quadrant best describes your organization?

SLOW DOWN TO IMPROVE RESULTS

Slowing down to get better results is not something that we are hardwired to understand. We live in a world where speed is king, faster is better, and organizations are constantly trying to accelerate what they do. However, sometimes it is important to slow things down to ensure that you are going down the right path and that you are getting the best possible results. Research in Motion (RIM), Toyota, and Best Buy provide useful examples.

Research in Motion and the Playbook

Research in Motion is a Canadian consumer products company best known for its Blackberry smartphones. In 2011, RIM decided to enter the tablet market; it introduced the Playbook, which was smaller than many of the other tablets on the market. The problem was that RIM was so eager to enter the marketplace that it launched a product that was not ready for public consumption. It sacrificed the quality of the product as it accelerated its speed to market.

The number of apps available, which has a direct impact on the number of units sold, was small; the operating system was full of glitches; and users needed to tether a cell phone to the Playbook in order for it to receive e-mail. As a result, RIM didn't sell many Playbooks and ended up dramatically reducing the tablet's price to get rid of inventory.

What if RIM had decided to hold off on launching its Playbook tablet until its quality was better? If it had waited, perhaps its stock price wouldn't have dropped by more than 80 percent since the beginning of 2011.

Toyota's Quality Issues

In 2008, Toyota embarked on a growth strategy to become the biggest carmaker in the world. This ambitious goal seemed achievable for a company that had had tremendous success in global markets and was considered to be one of the best-quality carmakers in the world, if not *the* best.

What happened? Toyota executed its strategy too well and grew too fast. Without realizing what was happening, it began to sacrifice quality for marketing reach. The quality of its cars declined; Toyota started to make mistakes because it didn't align its growth strategy with its quality efforts. It focused only on the question, "How do we sell more cars?" and didn't consider how that increased volume would impact the quality of those cars. This strategy led Toyota to recall more than 15 million vehicles between 2008 and 2012.

A slower pace of growth would have allowed Toyota to continue to expand, and the company could have matched its quality efforts with its growth ambitions by hiring more quality-control resources. If it had allowed its quality processes to catch up with its pursuit of sales volume, Toyota might have avoided many of these quality issues.

Best Buy's Employee Turnover

One of North America's largest electronics chains, Best Buy, sells a wide range of products from printers and computers to TVs, cell phones, and cameras. Retail companies like Best Buy rely heavily on frontline employees; customers interact directly with them. Many potential customers make buying decisions based on the help (or lack thereof) that they receive while shopping in the stores.

Over the past few years, Best Buy has had an employee turnover rate that is consistently more than 40 percent. Although turnover rates in retail tend to be higher than in most industries, 40 percent is still a staggering number. Imagine losing almost half of your staff every year. Think of the time and money required to attract and hire people. Obviously, there was a problem: Either the right people weren't being attracted to the organization, or the hiring process was somehow skewed toward hiring people who would not stay with the company.

What if Best Buy had taken more time to hire the right people? What if the company had profiled the right type of employees and then recruited them? What if it had targeted specific people for specific roles? This would not only have helped attract better people but would also have made the process of employee retention easier. The best retention strategies begin at hiring.

HOW SPEED IMPACTS PROFITABILITY

How can managing speed impact profitability? Simple. Speed can make profits go up or down depending on how fast you go.

It may sound counterintuitive, but sometimes slowing down how we operate will increase profitability.

As a specific example, one of my clients, a bank, wanted to implement a new technology system across numerous departments. Many different stakeholders were involved, all with their own interests that needed to be met. The initial plan was to implement the system quickly to replace old, manual processes. However, we decided that it would be best to gain support for the initiative before rolling it out to the various stakeholders. So, instead of pushing the initiative through quickly, we took the time to meet with stakeholder groups and departments within the bank, gather their feedback, discover how they were currently getting their work done, and then develop internal champions who would support the initiative.

Although the implementation took two months longer than originally hoped, the results were tangible. Stakeholders began using the new system immediately, very few changes were needed, and my client was able to achieve the expected savings from using the system much sooner than planned. This implementation became a blueprint for future change initiatives within the organization. In this case, slowing down the process helped make the change sustainable and made the best use of the resources available.

Figure 7-2 looks at the strategies and activities that many organizations employ and shows, in each case, how speed can have an impact on profitability. Let's look at three of the correlations on the diagram to better explain the relationship between managing speed and increasing profitability.

Strategy 1: Implement Strategy and Change. To effectively implement a strategy or change initiative, you need to slow down to ensure that it is done right. If my banking client had tried to move too fast,

Figure 7-2. How Managing Speed Increases Profitability

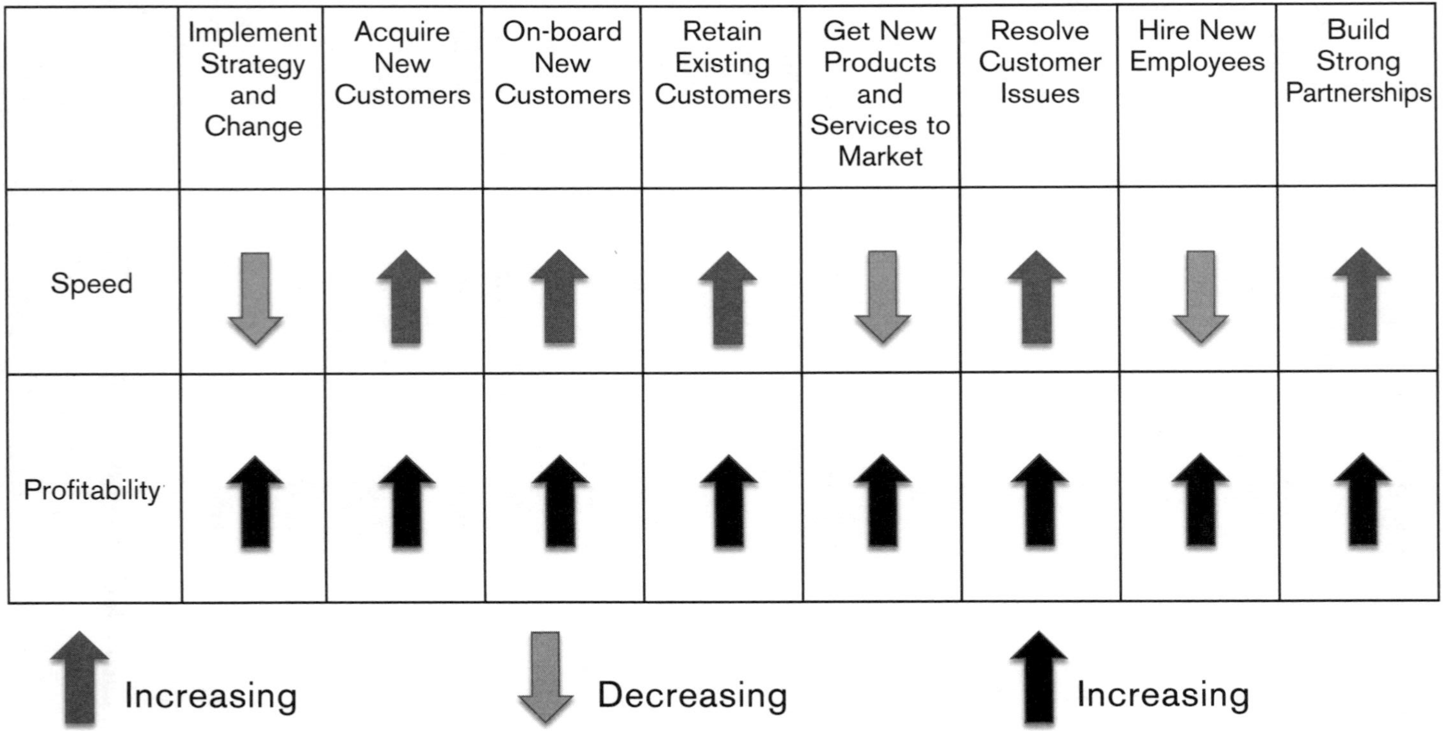

	Implement Strategy and Change	Acquire New Customers	On-board New Customers	Retain Existing Customers	Get New Products and Services to Market	Resolve Customer Issues	Hire New Employees	Build Strong Partnerships
Speed	→	←	←	←	→	←	→	←
Profitability	←	←	←	←	←	←	←	←

← Increasing   → Decreasing   ← Increasing

the change would not have been sustainable. In my experience, organizations can require up to three times more resources and time to resolve an issue after the fact than if they had prepared for it properly in the first place. Reducing the speed at which you roll out a strategy to ensure that you have the proper accountabilities and support increases your performance and allows you to focus on activities that add value to the organization.

Strategy 2: Acquire New Customers. When acquiring new customers, you want to accelerate the process and acquire them as quickly as possible without sacrificing the quality of the relationship. By shortening the process, you are able to reduce the cost of acquisition for each new customer, approach more customers to grow your base, and generate revenue faster from those new customers.

Strategy 3: Hire New Employees. When hiring and recruiting new employees, you need to slow the process to ensure that the right people are being hired. Making the right hiring decision leads to a reduction in the cost of hiring (which can be substantial, especially when hiring for executive positions). Besides freeing up key resources that can be applied to other value-added activities, a slower hiring process actually improves employee retention; you will be hiring more people who are the right fit for the organization.

> Look at the different functions of your organization and determine whether results might improve by speeding up or slowing down. Then take steps to adjust the speed accordingly.

THE SPEED–PROFITABILITY CORRELATION AND THE FOUR COMPONENTS OF OPERATIONAL EXCELLENCE

Let's see how each of the four core components of operational excellence is impacted by speed.

Attracting and Retaining Top Talent

Retention starts with hiring. The fastest way to retain the best people is to hire the right people in the first place. Organizations should be slow to hire, especially for key positions, and quick to fire.

Slowing down the hiring process allows you to ensure the right fit for key positions in your organization. Too many organizations have high turnover rates and spend too much money on hiring and rehiring because they don't take the time to ensure that they hire the right candidate the first time.

To avoid this, here are some steps to consider (which were expanded on in Chapter 3):

- **Develop different hiring processes for different roles.** You want to recruit specific candidates for key positions and *accept applications* for repetitive roles or those requiring a specific set of skills.

- **Focus on outcomes, accountabilities, and results, not on activities.** Most organizations write job descriptions that focus on experience and specific activities when they should be focusing on what accountabilities and results the role is expected to deliver.

- **Prepare for the process to take longer than expected.** If you have contingency plans in place so that your organization can still function effectively while it's searching, you can take the time to find the right person. Succession planning and cross-training for key roles are two ways to help provide stability during the hiring process.

Employee retention begins from the moment candidates become interested in working for your organization. The faster you can create an emotional connection, the more likely it is that they will want to work for you. Be slow to make an offer but quick to engage new employees and to strengthen their connection to the organization. Make them feel comfortable and confident in the decision they made to join your organization.

A large Canadian not-for-profit hospital foundation had been through three presidents in four years. The result was poor morale, high staff turnover, and frustration on the part of donors because of a lack of stability in how the foundation was run.

The board of directors, in conjunction with the hospital president and CEO, implemented a different process as they started the search for a new foundation president. This process would be slower and more deliberate to ensure that they filled the position with the right person. The board engaged key stakeholders and developed a candidate profile that listed the ideal characteristics and accountabilities for the position.

The organization then went out and looked for people who fit the profile. Instead of asking people to apply, they recruited specific candidates. After six months, a new president was hired with the approval of all key stakeholders. The organization had taken the time to determine the characteristics the right candidate should possess and had engaged key stakeholders for early support, in contrast to the previous hiring processes, which were focused purely on speed.

Innovating and Collaborating

Innovation can mean an enhancement to an existing product or service or something that is brand-new to the marketplace. For the purposes of this book, I define innovation as any enhancement that improves outcomes for customers.

When you are developing an innovation, it is important to move quickly, but it is also important to develop an enhancement that will work and that can have an impact. When developing an enhancement to an existing product, there is an advantage to rolling it out quickly. When determining how quickly to develop and roll out any innovation, consider these key questions:

- ◆ Does the market need this, or are you developing something that has not yet been contemplated?
- ◆ What are the barriers to adoption for this innovation?
- ◆ What are the advantages, if any, of bringing this innovation to market first?
- ◆ What are the risks of bringing the innovation to market too quickly?

The answers to these questions will help dictate the speed at which you should operate. The more disruptive the innovation, the more you need to slow down to ensure that it is rolled out properly.

The development of patented pharmaceuticals is a classic balance between speed and quality. The advantage of being first to market with a patented drug is enormous, but, to do that, the drug must not only be developed, it also must pass a litany of tests. Move too slowly, and a competitor will bypass you. Move too fast, and your drug may not be approved for use.

Lipitor, produced by Pfizer, was approved for use in 1996, and the patent expired in 2011. During that time, Lipitor exceeded $125 billion in sales. What is interesting about the story is that Pfizer did not come up with the first drug to lower cholesterol; Merck did. And Merck actually did it twice. Each of its drugs, Mevator and Zocor, had more than $1 billion in sales before Lipitor entered the market. And Pfizer did not even develop Lipitor; it was developed by Warner-Lambert, which Pfizer purchased.

How did Lipitor become so successful? Pfizer provided better clinical results than the other drugs on the market, and it developed and executed the right marketing plan. It focused on ensuring that the right people supported the product. At every turn, Pfizer was told it could not dominate a market already established by Merck. But it took the time to speak with the people who would be giving its product to patients: doctors. In fact, Pfizer developed a strategy that turned doctors into ambassadors for Lipitor. A major selling point was that patients could start with a lower dosage, thus reducing the risks of side effects, yet would see a higher reduction in their cholesterol levels. It was a win-win.

Lipitor was so successful because Pfizer didn't rush to market; it didn't try to be first or catch its competitors. It took its time to find the right strategy and focus on the differentiating factors of its product. Today, Pzifer can point to 125 billion reasons why this strategy was successful.

Aligning Strategy and Tactics

One of the keys to any successful strategy implementation is the alignment of tactics (operational activities) with the future vision to be achieved (the strategy). Remember that strategy is the what and tactics are the *how*. How something will be achieved must be aligned with what needs to be achieved.

When organizations try to implement their strategy too quickly, they usually fail because they haven't taken the time to ensure that their activities are aligned with their vision. Organizations should default to a slower implementation process to ensure that a strategy can be sustainable and that appropriate support can be gained. Your speed in implementing a strategy is determined by your ability to ensure that these items are in place:

- ♦ Support for the strategy at all levels of the organization
- ♦ A measurement mechanism to track results. And be sure to track results, not activities
- ♦ A single person is accountable for the success or failure of the strategy
- ♦ An implementation plan has been developed

The faster you are able to create the right foundation for implementing the strategy, the faster you will be able to align your tactics with that strategy. In this case, quality is more important than speed because you want to ensure that the strategy is implemented effectively from the get-go.

The next time you engage in a strategy development process, think about accelerating the development of the strategy and slowing its implementation in order to get the best results.

When Frances Hesselbein ran the Girl Scouts of America from 1976 to 1990, noted management consultant Peter Drucker commented that it was one of the best-run organizations in the world. This was because its tactics always aligned with its strategy.

Before Hesselbein took over the organization, it had not been very diverse in its membership. She wanted to change that. She felt that, to effectively increase diversity within its membership, she first needed to increase the diversity of her management team and the organization's board of directors.

Once that diversity was accomplished, the organization developed marketing materials for each of the ethnicities it wanted to target. Posters depicting girls from different cultures engaged in activities that aligned with their cultural beliefs were developed and distributed. Communications were developed to target the various ethnicities by speaking directly to the parents, showing how their daughters could maintain their cultural ties and still grow and develop and become part of a great organization.

The development and execution of tactics like these allowed the Girls Scouts to more than triple its racial and ethnic diversity in a short time. The tactics were directly aligned with the organization's strategy and future vision.

Acquiring and Keeping the Customers You Want

Getting your customers to become ambassadors for your brand is the quickest way to grow your business. Your customers are already familiar with your products and services, and they know the level of quality and value you provide. The faster you can turn customers into brand ambassadors, the faster you can grow.

Though it's important to engage your customers quickly, it's much better to engage them before they even become customers. The customer on-boarding process (your process for bringing on new customers) provides a tremendous opportunity to engage new customers and show them how important they are to you (as discussed in Chapter 6).

I am part of a global community of consultants started by management consulting guru Dr. Alan Weiss in 1996. His vision was to build a community of like-minded consultants to share their best practices about business and life. These consultants have become Dr. Weiss's customers through a variety of offerings that he provides to help them grow their consulting businesses and improve their lives.

This community was developed so successfully that it became a lab for Dr. Weiss to test new ideas and offerings and to solicit input directly from customers. Through an active online forum (www.alansforums.com) and regular in-person events, he has not only engaged the members of his community; many of the ideas for his new offerings come directly from its members. And these are not just ideas. In many cases, members of the community have become strong ambassadors for his brand and help recruit others to participate in these new offerings. By creating these ambassadors, Dr. Weiss is able to acquire new customers and generate repeat business very quickly.

A perfect mix of value and a sense of community has brought together customers from around the world who help each other grow both personally and professionally. At the same time, they provide value to Dr. Weiss and other community members.

THE MYTH OF THE FIRST-MOVER ADVANTAGE

Business schools all over the world teach us about the so-called first-mover advantage and the benefits of being the first to market with a particular product or service. The basis of the first-mover advantage is this: The company that is first to enter a new market gains an advantage over both current and future competitors. We are told that this advantage leads to the ability to hold on to significant market share. But it is simply not true.

Why There Is No Advantage to the First-Mover Advantage

There is no advantage to being a first-mover. This may seem counterintuitive; there should be advantages to being first to market with a product. After all, being first to market with a newly patented pharmaceutical product can mean years of domination; even then, however, you are the *only* mover, not the first-mover. In most cases, there is a dearth of evidence to support the theory.

Apple didn't invent the tablet computer; Microsoft did. Yet Apple has more than a 50 percent market share. General Motors didn't invent the first affordable car; Ford did. Yet GM has almost 20 percent of the North American market share. Google didn't invent search engine technology; WebCrawler did. Yet Google controls almost two-thirds of the search engine market. Intel didn't invent the computer microchip; Texas Instruments did. Yet Intel is the top producer in the world of computer microchips. Disney didn't invent the concept of theme parks, yet more than 130 million people visit its parks each year.

These companies didn't worry about the idea of first-mover advantage. In fact, they were happy to let someone else enter the market first and make all the mistakes first-movers make. They saw what worked and what didn't, and they identified gaps and opportunities on which they could capitalize.

> It doesn't matter whether you are first to market. What matters is your ability to leapfrog over the competition once you arrive.

What makes such companies so good at negating the supposed first-mover advantage? Here are just a few reasons:

+ They see opportunities and gaps in the marketplace and are flexible enough to pounce on them.

- They ensure that those opportunities align with their core business strategy and organizational strengths.

- They are able to find areas of competitive advantage (speed, quality, functionality, distribution, customer experience) and leverage them.

- They have the discipline to effectively execute their core business strategy and not be distracted by other opportunities.

- They are able to create a unique experience that draws customers closer to them.

- They are able to calibrate the speed at which they operate, knowing when to speed up and when to slow down.

Effective execution and the pursuit of operational excellence play a more important role than being first to market. The ability to leap over your competition is a much stronger advantage than how fast you get to market. When someone else is first to market, strong companies see how the market responds and make improvements to their offerings to create exponential growth and erect barriers between themselves and the competition.

First-mover companies expend a great deal of energy getting there first, while the competition waits patiently for the opportunity to strike.

Great race car drivers sometimes follow closely behind other drivers in the first few laps of a race to see the nuances of the course and the other drivers' strategies. This approach, called "drafting," saves energy and resources and allows the drivers to make up speed. Once they are comfortable, they can focus their effort on taking control of the race because they have seen where taking a sharp turn too quickly or passing too high on the track can lead to mistakes. They have also determined the best places to overtake the competition.

First-mover advantage works only if you are the first person in line when they are giving away free iPads, but not if you are the company that makes them.

Perhaps your strategy to be first will only make you finish last.

Alternative Strategies to Consider

How you choose to grow your organization will dictate the speed at which you can move. The first-mover advantage is not really an advantage; you should be spending more time on developing ways to implement the right strategy for growth.

Figure 7-3 shows four possible strategies to grow your organization. (This visual was originally developed by Dr. Alan Weiss; I have changed the labels to suit the purposes of this book.)

Status Quo. When you adopt this strategy, you continue to offer your existing products and services to current customers. Because you are already established with these customers, you should be able to move quickly, but there is very little opportunity for significant growth.

Value Add. This strategy involves offering new products and services to current customers. Because these customers already know your organization and its offerings, you don't need to worry about the cost or timelines of customer acquisition. However, you do want to ensure the quality of your new offerings; you need to be certain not only that your customers will purchase them but that they will also continue to purchase your existing products and services. You can move quickly because of the existing customer relationships, but you must be mindful of quality.

Growth. When you utilize this strategy, you offer your existing products and services to new customers—that is, you move into a new market with them. Because you already have existing products and services and other customers who are using them, you can do this quickly; you can use existing customers and other members of your network to make introductions and provide referrals.

You don't want to move too quickly because you need to consider the issue of capacity: How many new customers can you take on without impacting the quality of your products and services or the quality of the relationship with your existing customers? Move at a reasonable pace and develop a plan that ensures quality.

Expansion. This strategy comes into play when you offer new products and services to new customers. In this case, the first-mover advantage is really a disadvantage. You need to be methodical when taking this approach. It is the one that provides the highest risk for the organization because you don't have an established product or an established customer base.

The more ambitious your growth plans, the slower you need to go to ensure that you take advantage of the opportunities in front of you. Determine which of these four strategies best suits your organization; then develop a growth plan for how you will achieve it. Always be mindful of your speed.

Figure 7-3. Methods of Growth

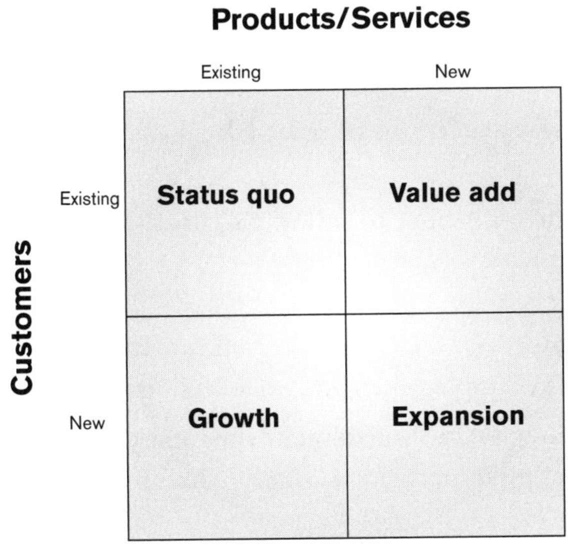

Products/Services

	Existing	New
Existing	**Status quo**	**Value add**
New	**Growth**	**Expansion**

Customers

KNOWING WHEN TO SPEED UP AND WHEN TO SLOW DOWN

Now that you understand why managing your operating speed is beneficial for your organization, you need to consider some key guidelines and leadership requirements.

Guidelines for Finding Optimal Enterprise Velocity

The following list is not exhaustive, but these guidelines should go a long way in helping you determine when you should speed up and when you should slow things down.

Here are some guidelines to follow to know *when to speed things up*:

♦ When the opportunity requires being one of the first to arrive in a particular market (for example, in the case of a niche market with a small customer base)

♦ When moving faster than the competition can be a competitive advantage (for example, when you need to bring on new customers)

♦ When you can accelerate profitable company growth (by, say, acquiring new customers)

♦ When you can leverage an existing market

♦ When an issue needs to be resolved

Here are some guidelines to follow to know *when to slow things down*:

♦ When quality has a larger impact on profitability than speed (for example, when you are building a car)

♦ When taking extra time to make the right decision can have a lasting impact (for example, when recruiting and hiring)

♦ When you need to make a complex organizational change as you enter a new market

How Strong Leaders Manage Speed

It takes a strong leader to slow an organization down when everyone else wants it to speed up. Leaders need to understand not only their own organizational culture but also the outside influences that impact results. Factors like the economy, government regulation, competition, commodity prices, shareholder concerns, and the environment can all impact the decisions a leader must make.

To best manage an organization that calibrates speed, leaders need to possess four attributes:

Adaptability. Leaders need to be able to lead in a variety of environments—a crisis, a boom, moderate success, ambiguity. They must be able to understand and then adapt to the environment and make decisions accordingly.

Perceptiveness. Leaders need to know what is going on around them, the personalities of the teams they lead, the agendas of each group of stakeholders, how they are perceived by others, and any external forces that can impact results. They can then use this information to determine how to best achieve the organization's goals and objectives.

Decisiveness. Leaders need to be able to balance their desire for consensus with the required speed of decision making. This also means knowing that, in most cases, some action is better than no action.

Humility. Leaders need to recognize that they require smart people around them and that they can't do everything on their own.

I will also let you in on a little secret. Great leaders aren't always at the top of their organizations. There are many great leaders we have never heard about, yet they show all these attributes. Do you know who those people are in your organization?

In Chapter 3, we looked at Michael McCain, CEO of Maple Leaf Foods, who helped his organization slow things down to improve results during a crisis. We also considered other leaders, like Sam Palmisano of IBM, who helped their organizations speed things up to take advantage of opportunities in the marketplace. These leaders were able to make the decisions to manage speed only because their organizations were flexible enough to support them.

IMPLEMENTING A CULTURE OF SPEED OPTIMIZATION

Now that we have all the tools required to foster a culture of speed optimization, we need to ensure that the culture we build will maintain it. Leaders must show the people in their organizations why a speed-optimizing culture is paramount to its ongoing success. This was covered in Chapter 3, in the section titled "The Key Principles of Leadership."

As with any change that is being implemented, your people must be able to answer the question, "What's in it for me?" People default to resisting change, so you need to overcome that behavior by appealing to the self-interest of each stakeholder group.

Here are some questions to consider as you set out to implement a new culture of speed optimization:

- How will optimizing speed impact our results?
- What can I do to show that progress is being made?
- What are the necessary performance indicators that will allow me to know when to speed up and when to slow down?
- How will speed optimization impact the daily activities of the different stakeholder groups? How will speed opti-

mization benefit them? Will they work fewer hours? Need to do less rework? Have reduced errors?

+ What is the best method for communicating this change?

+ Whom can I enlist to help implement the change?

+ Who will be the biggest dissenters, and how will I approach them?

+ What are some of the roadblocks I can expect to encounter, and how will I tackle them?

+ What will this organization look like when we have achieved the right culture, and how will I communicate that vision effectively?

There are many more questions to consider as we embark on implementing a complicated change initiative. The important thing to ponder is how it will impact the people in your organization.

Operational excellence is not a destination; it is a mind-set. It is focusing on ways to improve the performance of the organization, and that needs to happen one person at a time.

CHAPTER 8

CENTERS OF EXCELLENCE: NOT SO MUCH

A FEW YEARS AGO, ORGANIZATIONS began creating centers of excellence that were meant to apply best practices to enhance a specific function of an organization. A center of excellence aims to improve results in that function throughout the organization.

A defining feature of the center of excellence is that it focuses on one function; it does not encompass all functions throughout the entire organization. Centers of excellence were created for functions like project management, procurement, quality management, and technology. Sometimes multiple organizations got together to create a center of excellence that answered to the needs of all the organizations, for such areas as research, safety, and even the arts.

We don't hear about centers of excellence so much anymore. That doesn't mean they don't exist; it's just not the trend anymore to call them centers of excellence. Maybe that was because the concept of a center of excellence was ridiculous. Organizations that were not able to be excellent in any one area thought that by using a catchy name and pulling some strong people together, they would be able to create a new entity that would achieve remarkable things.

I have often wondered what the difference is between a center of excellence and simply centralizing a function within an organization or creating a shared services model. If an organization decides to centralize, say, all its procurement functions within one department, why wouldn't that be a center of excellence? Presumably, the organization would want that central procurement department to use best practices and to share those best practices across the entire organization so that everyone could take advantage of them. Also presumably, the organization would want that centralized procurement department to achieve the best results possible. So, really, a center of excellence is no different from creating a centralized function for something within the organization, which also fits into the shared services concept.

The biggest problem with centers of excellence is that organizations believed that just by calling them centers of excellence, they would be excellent. They didn't understand the amount of work that goes into not only creating a center of excellence but also in maintaining that excellence. That's where most centers of excellence failed.

More importantly, why would organizations focus on excellence in only one area? Why not try to make every department in an organization excellent? The ability to pursue and achieve excellence across an entire organization separates the best companies from the rest, not just to excel in one function or area. After all, if an organization is able to make one area excellent, it should be able to also

Successful organizations don't focus only on making one department excellent. They focus on excellence across the entire organization.

achieve excellence across its other areas. It really makes no sense to pursue excellence only in one "center."

WHY CENTERS OF EXCELLENCE AREN'T ALWAYS EXCELLENT

Centers of excellence can't be set up and then left to run on their own. Like any department or organization that pursues operational excellence, centers of excellence should be set up to continue to improve, enhance, and innovate. Think of them as mini companies.

But as soon as a center of excellence stops adding value to the organization, it becomes a center of wasted time and resources. A true center of excellence is constantly improving how it operates, is constantly finding and implementing new best practices, and is constantly adding more and more value to the organization.

What Organizations Do Wrong

Back when centers of excellence were all the rage, the most common mistake an organization made after it created one was to quickly forget about the word **excellence**. They began with the best intentions—bringing together the best people from within the organization and establishing best practices—but after a while they tended to stop focusing on improving the center, instead allowing it to run on its own.

Centers of excellence went into autopilot mode, the metrics for success were not always aligned with the direction in which the organization wanted to go, and organizations forgot about the constant pursuit of excellence. Usually centers of excellence were effective at the outset, but they often lost effectiveness as time went on. As people settled into their roles, they began to focus on performing activities instead of driving results. They stopped looking for ways to improve and got comfortable performing repetitive actions. They began to perceive other departments looking for guidance as nuisances, not customers or business partners, and other departments began to perceive them as compliance people.

Consider the finance or marketing functions within your organization. They are likely centralized for the entire organization, at least to some degree. How do you think of them? Are they a support function or an annoyance that you need to deal with? I bet if we took a survey, the responses would be evenly split between negative and positive. The problem with so-called centers of excellence is that they work only if the people running them take the right approach.

Building a center of excellence is not just an event with a powerful-sounding name; it is an ongoing process that needs to be constantly addressed and updated. But often, as organizations achieved initial success with this approach, they forgot why they were successful and started just maintaining the status quo. Centers of excellence were usually started around a specific issue of importance to an organization, so short-term needs usually superseded longer-term objectives. In many cases, this meant that the activities being performed were not always in the best interest of the long-term success of the organization.

A center of excellence often had no clear metrics for success— another reason the activities it performed didn't always align with the corporate direction. Again, employees will generally behave as they are measured. Organizations often used the same metrics for the centers of excellence as they did for other departments, rarely looking at the return on investment. So why would they expect the results to be any different?

Organizations had a poor understanding of the culture change required to maintain excellence and gain support for effective processes. They focused on the activities and the processes, but they did not implement a culture and mind-set for excellence. The focus was on short-term gains, often at the expense of more dramatic long-term results. As we know, the ability to change an organization's or even a department's mind-set is of paramount importance if an organization is to be successful.

The bottom line is that organizations tried to create centers of excellence in which things were different. But it was really only a conceptual gesture. There is no reason to believe that an organization that is mediocre in many areas will be able to sustain excellence is one area. And if it could do that, why would it stop with that one area? Why not instill that culture of excellence across every department? That is the fundamental flaw in the center of excellence concept.

Why You Should Avoid Centers of Excellence

Another mistake organizations make is creating a center of excellence when there is really no benefit to doing so. Centralizing certain functions within an organization or across many organizations doesn't always make for improvements. Organizations need to remember that the results and accountabilities of a center of excellence have to improve the way an organization operates, not make it more difficult.

Later in the chapter, I will pose some questions to consider before you set out to create any form of centralized department or organization—although, again, you are better advised to focus on creating excellence in every area of your organization.

So, first, here are some situations when the centralization of activities into one department may not make sense:

- ♦ When you have a global organization and the operating processes and regulations are very different from one country to the next
- ♦ When the decentralization of a particular function or set of activities will yield better results
- ♦ When you don't have the right capabilities and can't hire the right capabilities in your employees

♦ When the incentive to create a centralized department is anything but to improve the performance of the organization

A Center of Mediocrity

A few years, ago, I worked with a client in the initial setup of a center of excellence. This center was to perform purchasing and contract management activities for multiple organizations. Many of the employees being hired for the center of excellence were from the organizations that would use it for their purchasing and contract management activities.

Our biggest challenge was that the center of excellence was not being created out of a need. The organizations that were to be a part of this center did not come up with this idea on their own; the idea came about because of financial incentives provided by the government. Essentially, the government was offering financial assistance to any entity created with the purpose of saving money through group purchasing and contract negotiations.

This challenge led to many roadblocks along the way. It was difficult to find the right people to run the center of excellence because such individuals needed to have not only a vision of the future but also the ability to manage diverse stakeholders. It was difficult to get progressive-thinking employees because many of the candidates came from the organizations that were going to use the center of excellence (the customers), so they had their own way of operating and often favored their own organizations'.

It was difficult to find common operating processes because the various organizations all did things differently. It was difficult to develop appropriate metrics because each customer organization had different goals and objectives. It was difficult to implement a culture of excellence because we were trying to bring together people who were not used to constant improvement and were comfortable in the way they had been operating for many years.

In the end, we succeeded because we focused on the principles of operational excellence and created the centralized department as a new organization, separate from the old ways of operating. Here are some of the things we did to maximize success:

- We hired a mix of people to work in the centralized department. Some of them came from the organizations that would use the center, and others came from outside those organizations and even outside the industry. This allowed us to breathe fresh air into how the organization was to operate.

- We created new operating processes that were not linked to any of the organizations. We took successful practices from inside some of the organizations and combined them with other successful practices from outside the organizations.

- We built a transition plan for employees coming from customer organizations to ease the burden on them. This provided a roadmap for who was to make the transition and when.

- We created an organizational structure that allowed for a great deal of support for the customer organizations to ease the transition to the new way of operating.

- We implemented a clear system of success metrics and regular performance review meetings with the customer organizations to ensure that business objectives were aligned.

- We encouraged employees to suggest new and better ways of operating so that we could foster a culture of change and innovation. This gave the employees ownership over what they were doing.

These success factors can be replicated across any organization and any department. They should not be applied only to a so-called center of excellence. They should be applied across your organization so that you can achieve excellence everywhere.

Let's get rid of the term *center of excellence*. It sounds great, but it has no practical application. We can talk in terms of centralizing functions where that makes sense, but we should no longer be talking about centers of excellence. We should be talking in terms of excellence across an entire organization.

I recently reached out to a group of colleagues from around the globe and asked for examples of great centers of excellence to use for this book. Not one of them had a good example. These are leading experts working with some of the most successful companies in the world, and no good examples came to mind. That alone is a good enough reason to get rid of the concept of centers of excellence.

Meanwhile, in some situations, an organization can successfully pursue operational excellence by creating one or more centralized departments. Let's start by considering three key reasons to create centralized departments.

WHY CREATE A CENTRALIZED DEPARTMENT?

If you are going to create a centralized department, you want to make sure you are doing it for the right reasons. We have seen what happens when centralized organizations are created with no clear objective in mind: They tie up resources; they frustrate customers and employees; they waste effort. For example, look at what is happening in the health care system in Alberta, Canada. Originally, the health care system was decentralized and was the responsibility of the different areas of the province. Then a new organization was created, and the entire health care system was centralized in order to gain more control and to save money. The province has now gone back to a variation of the previous model by decentralizing some power to five regional health authorities. Most recently, many members of the board of directors were dismissed, and the

CEO was fired, along with about 20 executives. So much for centralization.

Make sure you know exactly why you are creating this centralized department and what you want the outcome to be. Is the purpose to lower costs by centralizing activities? Is it to increase collaboration across multiple organizations? Is it to leverage one country's ability to get better results? As with any good strategy and implementation, centralizing a function within your organization needs to start with the right objective.

There are some common reasons why organizations centralize activities and why certain functions are best achieved through centralized departments. Most such departments are created to help organizations improve in at least one of three important areas.

Governance and Oversight

One reason to create a centralized department is to provide governance and oversight for key initiatives. This is different from providing project management support. It is actually providing compliance and oversight to support initiatives that have higher risk to the organization and that require a different kind of oversight.

This governance and oversight support can be legal, financial, or related to compliance. The departments are staffed by legal and regulatory experts, as well as business and risk managers, to ensure that key initiatives across the organization are given the proper amount of attention. Such departments work well for global initiatives where the legal and compliance requirements are different across various countries but the management of the overall initiative must be centralized to ensure that the expected results are achieved.

Guidance and Support

Another reason organizations centralize activities is to provide guidance and support for the rest of the organization. In these instances, the centralized department is responsible for training the entire organization in the best practices to be used when it performs certain functions and activities. Those best practices are developed from both internal and external practices and brought into a new way of operating for the organization.

Those working in the centralized department are then responsible not only for using those best practices but also for rolling them out to the entire organization, as appropriate. The centralized department provides central direction on the practices to use, develops and rolls out training materials and communication tools to ensure that people throughout the organization are using those practices, and provides ongoing support by acting as the experts when employees have questions or issues to be resolved.

Results Tracking

A third reason to create a centralized department is to track activities undertaken toward a common goal and to measure results. In many cases, these departments are set up as project management offices (PMOs) that track key projects across the organization and provide project management best practices. These PMOs are responsible for developing project management best practices and rolling them out across the organization. But they are also responsible for tracking project activities and sometimes even results in order to ensure that key projects stay on schedule and on budget.

These departments are staffed by project management experts and finance specialists to ensure that the projects stay honest. These specialists either manage the projects themselves or provide key

> When considering the centralization of functions, you must clearly articulate their purpose and how the organization will benefit from the centralizing. And remember that standardization is not always a benefit to an organization.

support to other project managers across the organization through coaching and providing tools that help achieve common goals.

THE BENEFITS OF A CENTRALIZED DEPARTMENT

There should, of course, be benefits to centralizing a specific function across an organization. As already discussed, you don't want to go through all of that time and effort if you aren't able to achieve better results. The following sections discuss some of the key benefits organizations achieve when they successfully create a centralized department.

Consistent Communication

Consistent messaging across the organization should mean that employees will need to spend less time trying to determine their roles. Direction will be clearer, and expectations will be set. Everyone in the organization hearing the same message goes a long way to creating common objectives because employees are able to easily determine their role in helping to achieve those objectives.

Common Processes

Implementing standard ways of operating across the organization—presumably common processes that are proven to get results—should result in improved performance. An organization that standardizes its operating procedures should be able to better focus its efforts on the activities that add value to the organization and on the outcomes that need to be achieved.

But be careful to ensure that standardizing common processes is the right move for your organization. Standardization doesn't always mean improved performance.

Improved Results

The results the organization achieves through the creation of a centralized department should be better than the results it would have had without the new department. The types of results may vary. They could be financial, including decreased costs to improve the bottom line. They could also be risk or compliance related, that is, to reduce the overall risks of the organization. Performance-related results would allow the organization to achieve more with less.

Figure 8-1 shows the key elements when creating a successful centralized department and how they interact with each other.

CENTRALLY LED, LOCALLY EXECUTED

The hardest thing for some organizations is to sustain the pursuit of excellence in one department, let alone doing so across the entire organization, but centralizing a specific function in some situations makes sense.

You need to be strategic about what to centralize and how to centralize it. Centralizing a function that is performed on behalf of an entire organization does not mean that the centralized department is able to force change or processes on other employees. It means that the organization will be able to achieve better results

Figure 8-1. The Value of a Centralized Department

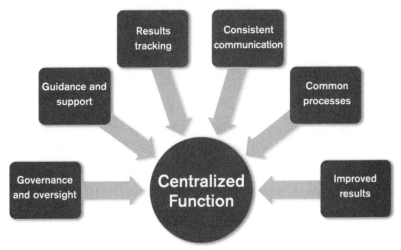

with a central group advising the rest of the organization on the best ways to operate.

If you are considering creating a centralized department (which, of course, will pursue excellence like the rest of the organization), here are some questions to consider:

- What is the objective of creating the centralized department? What are the expected outcomes?
- What are the implementation considerations? What impact will there be on the rest of the organization?
- Where will the employees come from? Should they come from inside the organization? Outside the organization? Outside the industry? Or some combination of the three?
- What success measures need to be in place to ensure that the expected outcomes are achieved?
- What will be the key accountabilities?
- Who will ultimately be accountable for success?

Once you have determined that the proper path is to create a centralized department, keep in mind these key success factors as you set up the new department:

- Provide central direction but leave some local flexibility in policies and guidelines.
- Provide guidelines and parameters, not strict rules. Trust your people to make smart decisions.
- Employees working in the centralized department need to be visible throughout the organization and build relationships with people in all areas. The centralized department needs to act as a group of experts, not as auditors or compliance officers.
- There needs to be a mind-set of growth, innovation, and performance improvement if the centralized department is to continuously improve and challenge the status quo.

♦ Technology needs to be scalable if it is to support the entire organization; it should be the enabler, not the driver of the strategy.

Remember the mantra "Centrally led, locally executed" whenever you are creating a centralized department; you need support and engagement from the rest of the organization. The centralized department needs to support the other parts of the organization and treat them as internal customers; its mission must be to provide these internal customers with a valuable service.

IGNORE THE CENTER AND FOCUS ON EXCELLENCE

Again, in most cases setting up a center of excellence is a recipe for failure. It sounds great in theory, but it rarely works, and it sends the wrong message to the organization. Setting up a center of excellence implies that only that one center should be excellent. Yet why shouldn't that same standard of excellence be applied to the entire organization?

Almost every center of excellence example I can think of was eventually a failure because of the reasons explained in this chapter. Let's forget the term *center* and create organizations and departments that run very well and achieve exceptional results.

One question organizations need to consider is, "If you can't make all of your departments excellent, why do you think you can maintain a level of excellence within just one center of excellence?" If you were able to maintain that excellence within one area, the so-called center of excellence, then why can't you replicate that success across the entire organization? Instead of focusing on creating centers of excellence, organizations should be focusing on achieving excellence throughout the organization.

Once you have a function or a department that is achieving operational excellence and great results, here are some questions that can help you replicate that excellence in the rest of the organization:

- ♦ What processes and practices are in place that allow us to be successful and achieve excellence?

- ♦ How are we measuring success? What does excellence mean for us?

- ♦ How are we empowering employees to make improvements?

- ♦ What structure is in place, and what leadership model is being employed?

- ♦ How have we aligned the activities being performed with the overall corporate direction?

- ♦ How are we encouraging collaboration among employees and business partners?

- ♦ What are we doing to encourage people to stay and continue to develop?

Success is great, but it's even better when you can perpetuate it. The key to consistently achieving dramatic results is to ensure that you focus on being the best in all areas of your organization, not just in one or two so-called centers. Leverage the areas where you are strongest. A focus on operational excellence throughout the organization is what will separate you from the competition.

Excellence in sales and marketing. Excellence in talent management. Excellence in customer engagement and retention. Excellence in strategy development and execution. Excellence in creating, producing, and delivering great products and services. These are the areas in which your organization should be striving. Eradicate the idea of creating centers of excellence, and focus on the idea of being excellent everywhere.

CHAPTER 9

INDUSTRY PERSPECTIVES

AS EXPLAINED IN CHAPTER 1, operational excellence is the constant pursuit of improved performance and profitability in all areas of your organization. It is about managing talent, driving innovation, aligning strategy with tactics, and enhancing customer engagement, all the while determining optimal enterprise velocity. It is about finding performance boosts in areas where you don't normally look.

Operational excellence is a mind-set, not a tool. It helps increase profitability, productivity, retention, engagement, empowerment, innovation, and many other drivers of an organization.

But operational excellence can mean different things for different industries. Some industries are more focused on people, whereas others need to focus on constant innovation. Still others rely heavily on processes and technology. In this chapter, I will discuss five key industries—retail, services, health care, technology, and manufacturing—and how an organization in each of these industries can move toward operational excellence. I will provide insights to consider if you are in one of these industries, along with an example of a company in each industry that is experiencing tremendous success.

RETAIL

In most retail organizations, frontline employees deal with the customers the most. Retail organizations generally deal with individual consumers, and when you deal with individual consumers, service and price become key factors in the buying decisions of those customers.

Retail organizations are competing not only against other physical organizations; they are also competing against online competitors. We often hear of consumers using a physical store to examine the details of a certain product and then going online or to the cut-rate competitor down the road to buy the product. Customers might use your resources to determine what they want to buy, but they might buy it elsewhere.

What you've got to do from an operational excellence perspective is to offer customers something they can't get elsewhere—not online and not in another store.

One of the things an Internet store can't provide is comfort and validation. Consumers who visit brick-and-mortar stores are often looking for comfort and validation about a decision. They want a recommendation from someone knowledgeable about their particular needs so that they feel they are making the right decision.

When consumers look at products online, there is less comfort and validation. Online retailers try to answer the need for validation with product reviews and testimonials. This is important, but it can't replicate the comfort level received when the customer can explain what he needs and an expert confirms that a certain product is right based on that specific set of circumstances. Retail companies need to employ and train knowledgeable, friendly staff who can make consumer recommendations and give consumers comfort that they're making the right decision.

As a retail organization, you need to look for the best frontline people; this is where one of the core components of operational excellence—attracting and retaining top talent—comes into play. It's not the executives at the top of the organization who deal with the customers. It's the people working in the stores who have the biggest impact on consumers' buying decisions. Make sure you're hiring people based on the values you're offering and that you want the customer to see. Attracting and retaining top talent is essential to any retailer's success.

> In addition to competitive pricing, retail organizations need to provide something consumers can't get online or in other stores—validation that they are making the right purchase based on their unique set of circumstances. Make customers feel comfortable about their purchases, and they will come back.

Obviously in retail there's high employee turnover because of seasonal shifts in the volume of business. But you've got to focus on hiring based on principles, not just on the availability of the people. You want to make your company the place top people want to work. Employing top talent as the face of the organization will lead directly to improvement in your sales.

Here are some key factors for operational excellence in retail:

- **An Effective Hiring and Retention Process.** Treating employees well and being the place where others want to work is essential to a retail organization's success.

- **Employees Who Are Strong at Relationship Building and Who Can Build Rapport Quickly with Different Kinds of Customers**. It helps dramatically when your employees are passionate about your organization and what it offers to customers.

- **Employees Who Are Empowered to Make Decisions That Are in the Best Interest of the Customer.** Power in retail organizations needs to be decentralized because organizations have only a few moments with a customer. How the employee behaves with customers will determine how loyal they become.

- **Employees Who Take Ownership for the Success and Failure of the Organization.** Retailers should establish a culture of accountability. With the empowerment to make decisions also comes accountability for the outcomes of those decisions. In organizations that encourage the resolution of customer problems and that don't punish productive failure, this accountability will increase.

- **Alignment Between the Strategy of the Overall Organization and the Tactical Work That Frontline Employees Do.** Employees need to know how their behavior can impact the direction of the organization so that they can perform in a way that is consistent with what is expected of them.

BMW and the Ultimate Customer Experience

I've chosen my own experience with BMW to showcase an example of operational excellence in retail. When I was in the market for a new car a couple of years ago, I decided to look at a BMW as one option. The experience (and I say "experience" because it was just that) began when I walked into a beautiful facility with lots of windows, state-of-the-art design, and, of course, mountains of beautiful cars. Nobody jumped on me as I walked through the door. I was permitted to wander for a few minutes before someone asked if I wanted some help. It was long enough for me to get comfortable in my surroundings, but not so long that I wondered if anyone knew I was there.

I was introduced to a nice man named Dave, and the first thing he tells me is that driving a BMW is like no other experience I will ever have. So I am intrigued. The conversation goes on, and I find out all about the features of the model I am interested in. Dave's presentation has a special focus on words like *performance* and *unique*. As I listen to him, I cannot believe that a car can do all these things. Then comes the kicker, Dave tells me that all service is included for the life of the car. This is not a huge dollar value necessarily, but a brilliant marketing move. I am drooling at the prospect of driving this car.

Then comes the test drive, the pièce de résistance. We pick up the car, and I enter the passenger side. Dave chauffeurs me around sharp turns and straightaways at speeds I did not think possible. I then think "Brace yourself!" as my driver slams on the brakes at 80 km/h (about 50 mph) with his hands in the air to show me the control the car maintains when braking.

It was then my turn to drive, but I was already hooked on the car. The paperwork was done quickly. I was introduced to the owner of the dealership and instructed to come back in a few days when a delivery manager would walk me through all the features of my car and help me set up my phone and any other devices. At this point of the story, I digress to identify why BMW exhibits operational excellence:

+ It offers customers a unique experience that makes each one feel special and at ease.

+ It hires employees who are both knowledgeable and passionate about the product.

+ Its corporate strategy and tagline are visible in every process the customer sees.

+ It knows its target customers and caters to them with a focus on great service and great performance, by both the car and the organization.

+ Employees are empowered to make decisions on the spot without going through a cumbersome approval process.

Remember that customers want to feel special; you need to foster an emotional reaction that pushes them to buy your products, not the competition's. Make them feel special; provide comfort, validation, and insight to help them make the decision. Give your employees the power to build a relationship with each individual customer.

SERVICES

The services industry is a hard one to tackle because it encompasses so many different types of businesses. It's everything from rental cars to consultants, from lawyers and accountants to landscapers and hotels.

A services business is a people-oriented business. In most cases, customers are not buying services; they are paying for trust. There are a million consultants out there, so the main factor in hiring one is reputation and trust. When you hire someone to take care of your children, trust is the main factor in the decision. When you choose an accountant or lawyer, of course, such a professional needs to have the requisite abilities, but you also need to trust that he or she has your best interest in mind. When staying at a hotel, you see and interact with the frontline staff and trust them to make your stay enjoyable.

Companies in the service business need to continue to develop relationships of all kinds. Those relationships will help you keep your existing customers and help you find new ones. Become the trusted source of information for relationship building by your customers.

Service organizations need to focus on building rapport and trust with customers because the relationships are often intimate and with individuals.

Here are some of the keys to operational excellence in the services industry:

♦ **A Focus on the Objectives of Your Customer, Not Your**

Own. Too many service providers try to drive their own agenda instead of the customer's. If you can align the two, that's great, but the focus needs to be on the customer's objectives.

♦ **A Constant Effort to Build Rapport and Trust with Your Customers.** Customer relationships in the service business are often very intimate, so trust is essential. I've often said that, for my consulting business, an organization pays me but an individual hires me.

♦ **Thought Leadership.** Great service companies are always bringing new insights and ideas to their customers and helping to improve the industry as a whole.

♦ **Having the Right People on the Front Lines and Allowing Them to Use Judgment.** As with the retail industry, in the services industry frontline employees are often the ones who deal directly with the customer. They are the face of the organization. Remember that when you are hiring, and look for people who are passionate about your organization.

♦ **Clear Communication About the Direction the Organization Wants to Go.** Employees must know how they can help drive the organization's strategy forward.

Four Seasons Hotels and Operational Excellence

Four Seasons Hotels and Resorts is annually ranked as one of the top organizations in the world in terms of service excellence. When Isadore Sharp founded the organization, he recognized that great service would be the differentiator for his hotels. Four Seasons has a culture of excellence. It is ingrained in every decision the organization makes.

Even though each of its hotels is unique and luxurious, the culture of excellence is prevalent. Four Seasons wants to ensure that the experience that guests have is easy and top-notch, from the time guests book a room to the time they leave the hotel. But it's more than just how the employees treat the guests. Four Seasons has the finest linens and the most comfortable beds. It has world-class spas and the softest pillows. When a new hotel is opened, no detail is overlooked to ensure that guests have the best experience possible.

Four Seasons was one of the first organizations to offer a teen concierge service—a service designed for the children of their guests. People staying at the hotel can use the concierge service to learn about activities in the area, what concerts and shows are playing, and other events that appeal to teens.

More recently, Four Seasons has launched a virtual concierge called Pin.Pack.Go at 77 of its 92 hotels. This virtual concierge is available online to anyone, even if they are not a guest of the hotel. Four Seasons is always looking for ways to improve the experience its guests have and to reach out to potential guests.

Here are some reasons Four Seasons is operationally excellent:

- Every employee who is hired must buy into the culture of service and excellence. They must put the guest first and exhibit pride and passion in working for the organization.

- Every decision an employee makes must have the customer in mind. The strategy to provide the best possible experience for the guest can be seen in the daily operations of the hotels.

- The organization is making itself an object of interest and an industry leader by providing value even to people who are not staying at the hotel through initiatives like Pin.Pack.Go.

- The organization is constantly looking to improve the way it operates, from back-end services that customers never see to frontline operations.

- Every hotel is unique, but the service provided in all hotels is expected to be the same. Four Seasons is able to sustain a culture of excellence across more than 92 hotels in 38 countries.

♦ Four Seasons empowers employees to use judgment and make decisions that are in the best interest of the guests.

Although staying at a Four Seasons hotel is an amazing experience for a guest, one can also see the pride that its employees take in working for the organization. That makes it easy for them to be engaged with guests and to make the experience for each guest a great one. Maintaining that culture of excellence has helped Four Seasons become a leader in the luxury hotel market.

HEALTH CARE

In health care, as in the retail and services industries, people are a very important factor in the success of organizations. For health care providers—hospitals, clinics, and other organizations—the people on the front line are nurses and doctors and even orderlies. Many people in many different roles interact with patients regularly.

In the health care world, patients are the customers, so every one of those interactions needs to be positive. It has been proven that, when patients feel comfortable and are treated well, they heal faster, they leave hospitals more quickly, and there is a reduced chance that they will return. So treatment of the patient becomes central to success.

To treat patients properly and give them the care they need, health care organizations need to optimize their performance in a lot of different areas. The best way to do this is to focus on solutions that have the greatest positive impact on the patient. The most important factors for operational excellence in health care are patient safety and patient outcomes. Everything a health care organization does needs to focus on the impact of a particular activity on the patient. This might mean looking at ways to reduce infection rates, developing a less invasive surgical procedure, decreasing wait times for key procedures, or discharging patients faster. The culture of improvement needs to focus on ways to improve the treatment of patients—the experience they have while they're being cared for.

> Every decision that health care organizations make should center on patient outcomes. They need to measure the real impact of their caregiving on the health of patients, not just on the number of days they spend in a facility or the cost of delivering standard care.

Even suppliers who deal with health care organizations can help by identifying areas where they can provide better solutions for their customers. When they focus on outcomes and results, solutions become easier to develop.

Here are some keys to operational excellence in health care:

- ♦ **Attracting and Retaining the Right People.** These not only have the right skills to give patients the best care but also have a passion for helping people get better.

- ♦ **Implementing the Right Procedures to Maximize Patient Safety.** Procedures to minimize infection rates and wait times, to speed the movement of patients and patient discharges, and many other factors that guarantee safety need to be in place to ensure a smooth operational flow and a minimum of problems.

- ♦ **Implementing and Sustaining a Culture of Empowerment, in Which Frontline Staff Are Empowered to Make Decisions in the Best Interest of the Patient.** Whether it's providing an additional pillow for comfort or moving the patient to a room with a view, employees need the ability to make important decisions without scrutiny or consequences. The key to implementing this strategy successfully is how the organization reacts when employees make mistakes because that will determine how employees will behave in the future.

- ◆ **Collaborating with Business Partners.** The most successful health care institutions collaborate with suppliers and other health care providers to find the best possible solution for the patient. The focus is on the patient's best interest, not that of the organization.

- ◆ **Implementing Technology to Seamlessly Share Patient Data and Information.** The most successful health care providers have technology that allows them to access and store key patient information so that it is readily available for employees. But it is also important that information can be shared with other organizations in the event that the patient arrives somewhere else for treatment.

Boston Children's Hospital and Operational Excellence

Boston Children's Hospital (BCH) is ranked as one of the top pediatric hospitals in North America in almost all of the key clinical specialties. It is viewed as a gold standard institution that other hospitals try to emulate. Over the past few years, BCH has made tremendous strides in the area of innovation. Because there are fewer pediatric hospitals than other types of hospitals, the market for solutions geared to pediatric hospitals is small; many medical device and other health care solution companies don't invest time or money in research for pediatric hospitals and instead focus on larger hospital opportunities and markets.

BCH management decided that much of the innovation they knew was needed would come from inside the organization, and they focused on how to best leverage the great people they had. When, as a first step, they hired a chief innovation officer, they became one of the only hospitals in the world to have such an officer on the executive team. They then developed an innovation program to encourage employees to become innovators. That program is having tremendous success.

Here are some reasons BCH is operationally excellent:

◆ They have implemented the Innovation Acceleration Program, which encourages employees to come forward with new ideas to improve the clinical performance of the hospital. The program has a separate evaluating committee, and the chosen initiatives are funded through a specific investment fund, the Innovestment Grant, set up specifically for the program.

◆ They have created a FastTrack Innovation in Technology (FIT) award that provides innovators with software development support for implementing new clinical software ideas.

◆ They hold a monthly Innovators' Forum in which they share stories about innovation that is taking place throughout the hospital. The presenters—doctors, nurses, and other clinical staff (called "innovators")—are the ones who actually developed the idea and took it through the piloting process.

◆ They hire employees who are not only the best at what they do but who also support a culture of excellence in which the patient is the focus. One of the commonly used mantras is "a relentless drive for excellence."

◆ They have access to and collaborate effectively with the Harvard Medical School and other organizations in the area.

◆ All new innovation ideas must be aligned with the hospital's strategic goals.

◆ They have developed a leadership development program in which speakers from both inside and outside the organization, and even outside the industry, provide unique insights on important subjects related to both health care and areas beyond the normal scope of health care.

◆ The employees who work in the Innovation Acceleration Program provide support to the people with the ideas (instead of coming up with the ideas themselves) and encourage them to come forward with new ideas. They are often referred to as "innovation facilitators" or "dream sherpas."

One example of an innovation that made it through the program and that won a FIT award is a mobile app called MyPassport, developed for patients and their families. The app tracks lab results, shows the plan of care for the patient, and allows the patient and family to send questions directly to the care team. It even has photos of the care team members. This app helps reduce patient anxiety, increases the transparency of the treatment plan, and builds stronger communication between the patient and the care team.

Focusing on patients and patient outcomes allows organizations to focus on the best solutions and those that are feasible. Organizations looking to thrive in the health care industry need to remember to focus and develop solutions and processes that support patients and that align with their organizational strategy.

TECHNOLOGY

The technology industry employs many prevalent delivery models, ranging from new to newer and the newest. There is software as a service (SaaS), what used to be called the "on-demand model." There are cloud services for accessing and storing data. There is software for analytics to tackle complex data. And there is technology we use every day to locate basic information or driving directions.

One interesting challenge for technology companies is that many of them have very little interaction with the end customer. If a customer is buying a software package or some form of online technology, the company selling that technology rarely, if ever, has a chance to directly interact with that customer. Even users of large technology systems rarely interact with the companies that sell them. So operational excellence for technology organizations needs to focus on managing how software is delivered to and accessed by the end customer so that customers can implement technology, integrate systems, and even download software easily.

Imagine being in an organization that sells products and services to one or two people, but then thousands of others use those products and services. How do you ensure a positive experience for all those users when you will never meet or talk to them face-to-face? Technology organizations need to develop new ways to reach and engage with customers remotely; then they need to figure out how to best leverage their customers and users.

The use of technology itself to do this can become a competitive advantage. Technology organizations need to be able to provide world-class customer service without ever meeting their end customers face to face. Their challenge is the opposite of that of retail companies.

Technology organizations have very little interaction with end users, so they need to develop seamless ways to deliver their technology to the people who use it and find other ways to create customer loyalty.

Technology companies have to deal with customer frustration. Technology is an enabler, one that people come to rely on and to resent when problems occur.

If you're a technology company, you want to help your customers find ways to self-diagnose and even resolve issues on their own. If you think about where technology is going next, it isn't necessarily about more touch points with the customer. The future will be in setting up fewer touch points with the customers and instead empowering them to diagnose and resolve their own problems. Empowering customers in this way will become a major advantage for the technology company that provides that kind of self-sufficiency.

Online chat features for technical support, virtual customer service representatives, even easy online help features that give the customer more control in solving their problems—whatever the vehicle—being able to diagnose and resolve those problems more quickly and more easily becomes a way to engage customers. That is how technology organizations use operational excellence to drive results.

Here is what some of the best technology companies do to pursue operational excellence:

- Identify a lot of new ideas, and turn the best ones into commercially viable products and services that help customers.

- Formally manage the innovation process and get new products and services to market as quickly as possible.

- Develop products and services that focus on solutions that anticipate or respond to customer needs.

- Have a clear vision of a technology roadmap for the future, and align their tactics and metrics for success with that vision.

- Help customers and users onboard by providing training and support in the implementation and use of new systems.

- Engage with customers remotely and in unique ways through support and tools to self-diagnose issues and resolve them quickly.

InfusionSoft and Operational Excellence

InfusionSoft provides sales and marketing software to small and medium-sized businesses. InfusionSoft is different from all other sales and marketing software companies because it offers the most comprehensive solutions. Their sales and marketing software contains various components—e-mail marketing capabilities, customer relationship management (CRM) capabilities, e-commerce capabilities, and social media capabilities. Other companies offer CRM capabilities, such as Salesforce.com. Other companies offer e-commerce capabilities, such as PayPal. And still others offer e-mail marketing capabilities, like iContact and Constant Contact. But none of these organizations offer all these capabilities in one solution. InfusionSoft does.

By integrating all these different capabilities, InfusionSoft has differentiated itself from its competition. The integrated software allows customers to manage the sales cycle electronically, from generating and converting customer leads to managing customer information to facilitating customer payments.

Here are some reasons InfusionSoft exhibits operational excellence:

♦ It found a gap in the marketplace and is able to exploit it.

♦ It is continuing to grow and innovate by anticipating (and even creating) what customers need next.

♦ It is using the very methods its software uses (social media, e-mail, the Internet) to increase its own brand awareness and acquire new customers quickly.

♦ It offers a plethora of online resources for customers and prospective customers. Articles, videos, and webinars are all available on its Web site.

♦ It continues to look for strategic acquisitions that align with its corporate vision.

♦ Because it offers a great work environment and great benefits for employees, it attracts and retains the best people. InfusionSoft receives thousands of job applications every week.

InfusionSoft has done a great job of creating a culture that fosters innovation and makes employees want to stay. Technology companies tend to be very good at creating environments where employees feel comfortable and can blow off steam (think of

Facebook, Google, and Intel, to name a few). The expectations of employees are high. They are expected to work long hours solving complex problems, so you'd think it would be difficult to retain them. However, technology organizations like InfusionSoft have found the right formula for getting tremendous results while fostering great company loyalty in its employees. Other industries could take some hints from successful technology organizations on how to build a culture in which employee retention is high despite the need to drive dramatic results.

MANUFACTURING

Manufacturing is a little different from the other industries discussed so far because the concept of operational excellence essentially started in the manufacturing world. The concepts of standardization and eliminating waste turned into methodologies like Six Sigma and Lean manufacturing (see Chapter 1 for more details on these concepts), which were adopted in some way by most manufacturing organizations.

Of course, those methodologies are not enough to sustain a world-class manufacturing facility. When we talk about manufacturing, we need to consider that technology is very important in the industry; in many cases, technology is taking over jobs that people used to perform. Quality becomes a very serious issue in manufacturing. Price is also an important factor because of the competitive nature of manufacturing in different areas of the world. Companies can always find a cheaper way to make the same products, but can they maintain their quality and management control? Manufacturing organizations need to find other areas of differentiation in which they can create competitive advantage.

Innovation is very important in manufacturing, and not just disruptive innovation. New products don't have to be ones that change an entire industry. Manufacturing companies can take huge advantage of incremental improvements that can become their point of differentiation. Manufacturing organizations have to start thinking about the design elements of what they produce. They need to think about how their customers use their products and what tweaks they can make to those products to attract more customers. Some people might call that *design thinking*, a concept started by IDEO (see Chapter 4). Manufacturing organizations should consider how to collaborate with key customers to determine what solutions are going to be the most valuable to them.

Lead times can be a very important factor in the success or failure of a manufacturer, along with quality. So is customer on-boarding—how organizations help their customers transition from where they are to using their products. What competitive advantages can your organization develop in these areas?

> Manufacturing organizations can increase excellence by collaborating with partners to determine how customers might use their products. Integrating a design element earlier will help manufacturing organizations differentiate with what they are producing.

Here are some keys to operational excellence in manufacturing:

- ◆ **Seamless Integration Between the Various Steps of the Supply Chain.** Products can be tracked all the way from the raw material stage until they are in the hands of the end customer.

- ◆ **Formal Management of the Innovation and Product Launch Process.** Products are launched on time, with the involvement of all the appropriate departments in the organization.

- ◆ **Collaboration with Customers and Suppliers to Make the Manufacturing Process More Seamless.** This includes sharing of data and demand forecasts to optimize the manufacturing process.

- ◆ **Processes That Maximize Results and Minimize**

Environmental Impact. This includes having manufacturing processes that have little to no carbon footprint and that encourage the recycling of any waste, as well as disposing of that waste in a way that doesn't harm the environment.

♦ **People Who Are Cross-Trained in Various Roles.** The aim here is to minimize downtime.

♦ **Processes and Procedures That Are Focused on Producing High-Quality Products and Maximizing Throughput.** Speed optimization is paramount; organizations know when they need to speed up and when they need to slow down in order to get the best results.

♦ **A Culture of Continuous Improvement.** Processes are constantly reviewed for enhancements.

♦ **Sales and Marketing Departments That Are Closely Integrated with the Manufacturing Process.** This ensures alignment between what is being produced and what is being sold to customers and pitched to potential customers.

Coach Inc. and Operational Excellence

Many of us know Coach Inc. because of its luxury handbags and leather accessories, such as wallets and luggage. What most of us didn't know is that Coach Inc. is one of the best manufacturers in the United States, at least according to *Industry Week* magazine. *Industry Week*'s criteria were mainly financial—profit margin, inventory turns, revenue growth, and return on assets. These criteria don't necessarily acknowledge excellence in manufacturing, but they do reward excellence in certain financial indicators that may be a result of strong manufacturing. I'm sure Coach Inc. isn't complaining about the distinction.

Here are some reasons Coach Inc. can also be considered operationally excellent:

♦ In response to growing demand for its products, it opened a new Asian division in 2010 to be closer to its Asian customers. Now it offers directly operated retail businesses in Asian markets, allowing it to gain better control of the management, quality, and lead times of its products.

♦ It consistently shows high inventory turnover, meaning it is able to control the cost of the storage and movement of goods.

♦ It is always looking to control its manufacturing cost base. In 2011, it moved some manufacturing out of China and into other low-wage economies.

♦ It works directly with factories and partners to offset higher labor costs by looking for increased efficiency, using lean manufacturing principles.

♦ It optimizes the speed of growth, instead of just focusing on going faster. In 2011, Coach Inc. chairman and CEO Lew Frankfort believed they could open twice as many stores profitably, but they didn't do so in order to stay focused on controlled growth.

Many people may think of Coach Inc. as a retail organization, but we also need to remember that it is a manufacturer. This essentially means that it pursues operational excellence in many different ways, whether with customer engagement at the retail level or with speed optimization at the manufacturing level.

Certain areas become more of a focus depending on the industry, but there is a great deal of overlap among the five industries examined in this chapter, which is why we can use a broad definition of operational excellence. When you consider managing top talent, innovating and collaborating, aligning strategy and tactics, and acquiring and retaining the customers you want, all coupled with optimizing enterprise velocity, the particular industry becomes less relevant. The core components of operational excellence apply to all industries.

CHAPTER 10

GETTING TECHNOLOGY OUT OF YOUR WAY

MANY ORGANIZATIONS VIEW TECHNOLOGY as the solution to all their problems. When they find problems in their operations, they sometimes seek, select, and implement a technology system that they think will make those problems go away. Technology companies fuel this course of action by touting all the great things their systems can accomplish. But organizations often forget one important point: Technology can't fix a bad process.

Technology can be used to improve and enhance operational excellence, but it needs to be used properly. This chapter discusses how organizations can effectively use technology of all kinds to improve operational excellence and achieve better overall results.

Let's start with the basic premise that technology supports operations; it doesn't drive them. Yes, we look at technology as something that can help us do things faster, better, and more accurately—maybe even with better cost-efficiency. But that does not happen by itself. The successful use of technology requires support by people, and people need to determine what the right technology is. People need to determine what outcomes need to be achieved. People need to use and maintain the technology once it's implemented.

The word *technology* encompasses a broad range of capabilities. Using a computer is technology. Using the Internet is technology. Using your smartphone is technology. But so is a robot that performs lab tests or a machine that packs boxes. These are all forms of technology. The essential question is, "How can I use technology to achieve better results more rapidly?"

FIX THE PROCESS, THEN IMPLEMENT THE TECHNOLOGY

One of the biggest mistakes organizations make is leading with technology. They discover a system that promises to make all their problems go away, they buy it, and they wait for the miracle to happen. But in most cases it doesn't happen. For an outline of how technology projects usually go, see Figure 10-1. The left side of the figure lays out a typical implementation process. Does this look familiar?

Too often we rush into finding a solution before we fix the root problem. My attitude when it comes to technology is that automating a bad process only allows you to make bad decisions faster. In my experience, that is the issue for most organizations. They believe that the technology will magically fix their operational problems. They forget that people have to actually use the technology. They forget that the technology needs to be implemented and likely integrated with other technology. They forget that asking people to use new technology means that those people must change how they operate. They forget that change is hard for most people.

A few years ago, a client purchased a new technology system to help manage their customs process for the importing and export-

Figure 10-1. A More Effective Implementation Process

A Typical Implementation Process

A company notices a problem and creates a list of requirements and specifications.

It finds a technology solution that meets those requirements and specifications.

It buys and implements the technology.

The technology fails or at least fails to live up to expectations.

People stop using the technology.

The company makes changes to the technology to try to increase usage.

A More Effective Implementation Process

A company sees an opportunity where technology can help improve results.

It identifies the outcomes and results that need to be achieved.

It identifies any impact on process and people.

It finds a technology system that supports the outcomes and results to be achieved.

It makes the necessary process and people changes, then implements the technology.

It measures success and makes additional operational improvements and technology enhancements.

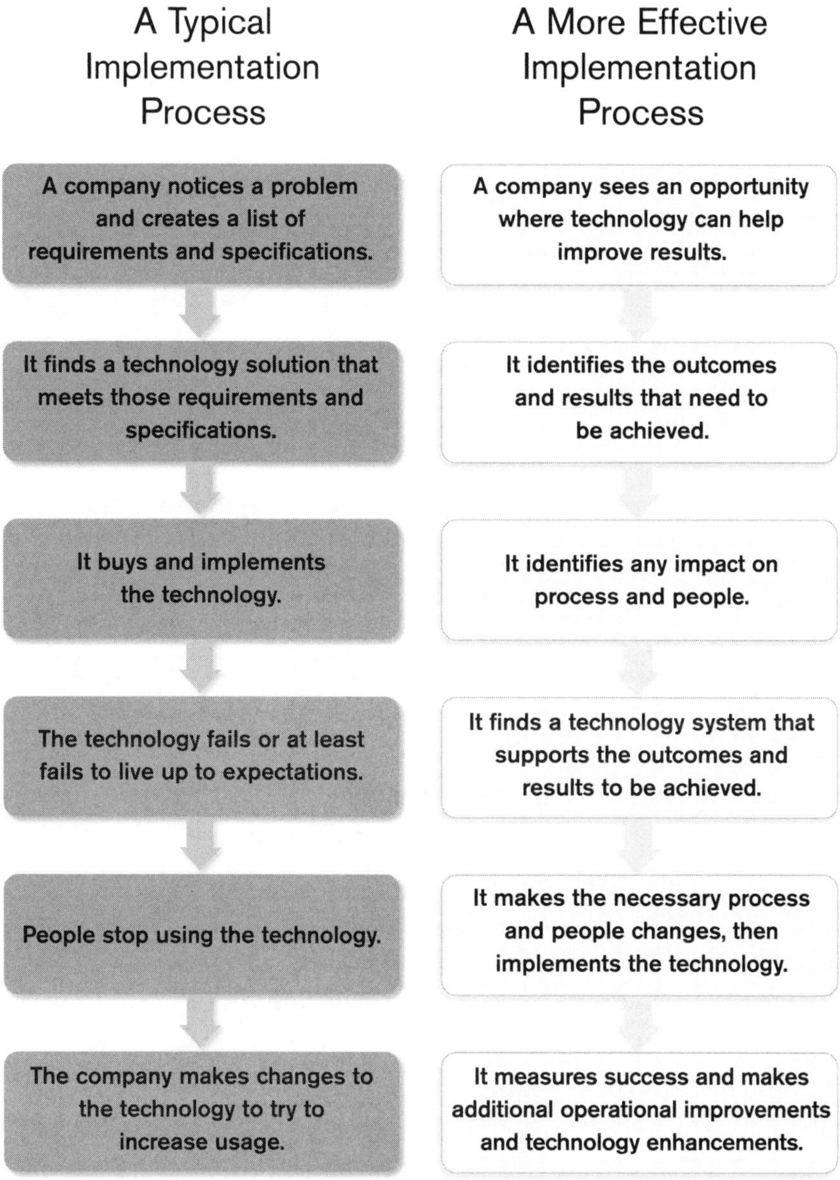

ing of goods. They rushed into a decision and purchased a system they hoped would solve all their problems. When I began working with them, I quickly realized that they had invested a great deal of money in a system that would not be suffi-

Organizations need to improve operations before they implement new technology. Otherwise they will automate bad processes, which only facilities the ability to make operational mistakes and bad decisions faster.

cient for what they needed. They had identified particular technical requirements and specifications that any such system needed to meet, and when they selected this particular system, they were confident it would meet their needs.

What was shortsighted about their process was that they didn't anticipate future needs. What if government regulations changed? What if they were to change the mix of products they import and export? Who was going to manage this complicated system?

After weeks of difficult conversations with leaders at all levels of the organization, I finally convinced them that they needed to change their strategy. Once they realized that they needed to focus on the outcomes that they expected the system to help them achieve and that the current system would not achieve those outcomes, we began to move in a different direction.

Their initial decision to buy the technology system had the right intentions but the wrong execution. They led with the technology and didn't take into account all the process and people changes that would be required for the technology system to work effectively. It was not an easy decision for them to change strategies. They had invested more than $1 million in the new system, and that investment would never be recovered. But they knew their costs would go even higher if they continued down the path they were on.

It is important to get technology right the first time and then to leverage that investment to achieve tremendous results. Look at the right side of Figure 10-1 to see how to run a successful technology implementation.

The biggest difference in the more effective implementation process is that the organization leads with an opportunity to improve performance and results, not necessarily with a problem that needs to be resolved (although that opportunity may manifest itself as a problem). The approach is different, and the impetus for using technology is different.

Let's look at my client who rushed into the technology decision and lost its investment. Let's give them a chance to turn back the clock and do things differently. What could they have done?

They should have started with the objectives of the department and the results they needed to achieve, which were to more accurately manage the customs process at a lower cost and to eliminate wasted effort. The first option they should have examined was whether they could make changes to their existing processes that would help to achieve their goals. Once it was established that there were better, more effective, and cheaper ways of operating, they needed to assess whether technology could help further those objectives, which in this case it could have.

My client should then have looked at how technology would impact the way they operated. They should have educated themselves on their technology options and even spoken with technology vendors to get a better understanding of the best solution for them. Once they knew what they needed to achieve, had a sense of the changes they needed to make and how those changes would impact the organization, and had collaborated with technology partners to find the best possible solution—only then could they select the appropriate technology.

My client would then embark on a partnership with the selected technology company and put in place a plan and success measures to ensure that their expectations and planning were aligned. Such an implementation needs to be structured so that both organizations are satisfied at the end. My client gets a new technology system that helps improve their performance and financial results, and the technology company gets a new client that is happily using their products and services and that can become a great referral source.

Here are some issues to consider as you contemplate the purchase of new technology:

Develop the Right Strategy. Before moving forward, you need to determine the right strategy for your organization. What objectives are you trying to achieve? What is your desired outcome? How will the company be better off? Do you have the capability to implement this system and the corresponding changes successfully?

Engage the Right People. As emphasized many times in this book, your strategy is only as effective as your ability to execute it. Make sure you engage the right people early and often so that they will own the initiative. Who are the key people who need to be involved in this decision and implementation? What skills are required?

Identify the Right Changes. You don't want to disrupt people's lives just for the sake of change. You want to work smarter, not harder; so identify the changes that will help improve the performance of the organization. Will the structure of the organization need to change based on any strategy changes? Will reporting relationships be different? Will people's job functions change? Will the processes you follow need to change in order to support the new technology? If so, are you improving the processes to achieve better results?

Develop the Right Tools. When implementing any change or new system, you need to develop tools that will help support the rollout for your employees. What are the areas that will experience the greatest impact? What support and tools can you develop to minimize the impact?

Measure the Right Outcomes. The only way to know whether you have been successful is to measure results. Those results and measures should tie back to the original outcomes that you wanted to achieve. How will you know if the initiative was a success? Who is ultimately accountable for that success?

Figure 10-2 lays all this out nicely. You start by developing the right strategy, but it's important to remember that strategy is organic. Hence the circular nature of the figure. You need to periodically revisit the strategy to ensure that it still aligns with the direction in which you want to go.

Technology can be a huge asset to an organization when it is implemented properly and for the right reasons. Adopting some of these tactics can help you do this successfully.

Figure 10-2. The Cycle of Successful Technology Implementation

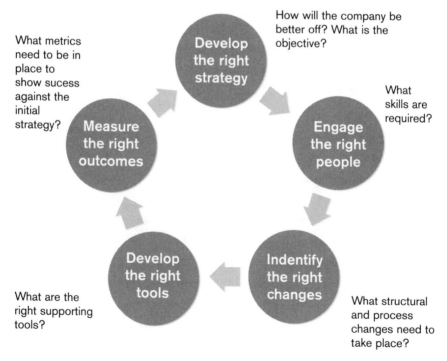

TECHNOLOGY AND CHANGE MANAGEMENT

Now I've done it—I have introduced the ambiguous phrase *change management* into the conversation. It's a catch phrase that everyone talks about but no one really understands.

Change management, or the lack thereof, is the main reason these projects fail. Companies implementing new technologies often forget about the amount of change that is required, even when they implement the simplest system.

Change management is not a soft skill or something only organizational development consultants should think about. It's a lot of work, and it can make or break any project.

Being successful in managing change doesn't mean just appointing a bunch of people and calling them a change management team. It means thinking through the impact that a technology implementation will have, how employees' jobs will change, and how to make the transition as easy as possible for the organization to absorb.

New technology changes the way employees do their jobs. Most people don't love change to begin with, but the issue is exacerbated when change is forced on people and when it affects what they do every day. You need to identify the impact the new technology system will have on the way people operate. You can't just strap a new technology system on top of what you already do.

Here are some tactics you can employ in rolling out a strategy that will ensure a successful technology implementation. This overall strategy is built on understanding the impact of the technology system you are about to implement and gaining support for it:

- Identify key stakeholders, and include them in the implementation planning from the outset.
- Identify the people or groups who will be most impacted by the technology, and have them help develop the new ways of operating.

♦ Look at other operating processes that are linked to the ones impacted by the technology, and identify how those processes will be impacted.

♦ Consider how the technology will change the data that is provided to employees, customers, and suppliers.

♦ Consider how any changes in operations will impact customers, suppliers, and other business partners.

Remember that when you implement new technology, it is not only the users of the system who are impacted. The implementation process often has a residual impact on people up- and downstream. Be mindful of how changing the ways one department, business unit, or division operates will impact other areas of the business.

One of my colleagues worked with a company to help them increase sales performance. The company changed their strategy for approaching customers and opportunities and implemented an improved technology system for tracking leads and prospects. The result was a 25 percent increase in sales within just six months. The only problem was that the manufacturing department was not brought into the initiative until after the new sales system was installed, and their processes were not coordinated with the data coming from the new system; they were thus unable to plan production to meet customer demand. Now the company faced a new issue: Deliveries were late to most customers. Sales were up, but customer satisfaction plummeted. The new sales system helped grow sales, but no one considered how key pieces of sales data would be communicated to the other areas of the organization that required it.

Implementing a new technology system impacts not only the users of the new system but also the departments and stakeholders connected to and dependent on those users and the data they generate.

USING TECHNOLOGY TO ENHANCE OPERATIONAL EXCELLENCE

Embracing the right strategy for implementing technology can have a very positive impact on your organization. Depending on the technology you implement, you may be able to do things faster and with less effort. You may have access to more data than you can use. You may reduce the duplication and errors inherent in manual work that's now been mechanized. You may even become more productive and effective in running your organization. How can technology enhance operational excellence? You'll see over the next few pages on the four components of operational excellence and the key factor of optimizing speed and explain how technology can enhance each one.

Attracting and Retaining Top Talent

Chapter 3 discussed some strategies for attracting and retaining the best people. It focused on ensuring that the people you are looking to attract are aligned with the direction in which the organization wants to go and are passionate about the products and services it offers. The ACM model for hiring (accountability, competency, and mind-set) was offered as a way to ensure that everything in your hiring is aligned properly.

Also discussed was how to retain your best people by giving them opportunities to take leadership roles on new initiatives, by setting clear expectations and accountabilities for them, and by recognizing their contributions to the organization's success. How can technology help us achieve all of those things?

EuroDisney is successfully using technology to reduce the risk and impact on the organization when top people leave and to better align the management plans of top people with their ambitions. EuroDisney completes an electronic profile for each of their top employees, and that profile is updated regularly with an employee's skills, accomplishments, and ambitions. The profiles actually take into account what each individual employee wants to achieve in terms of his or her desired development and desire to move up or around within the organization.

EuroDisney also creates job responsibilities and accountabilities for each of its top positions, then uses technology to match top employees to those positions. This has led to improved succession planning for key roles and improved bench strength within the organization, as well as helping the company retain a lot of its top people.

A recent start-up, Gild, is using the power of technology and data to liberate hiring teams from the challenges of finding top software developers, a group that is in huge demand. Gild has developed an algorithm that can evaluate the capabilities of millions of developers. Gild found a gap in the market when it realized how difficult it was for companies, especially those in Silicon Valley, to find the best developers. Their technology scours the Internet looking for clues on each developer, based on some basic questions: Is his or her code well regarded by other programmers? Does it get reused? How does the programmer communicate ideas? How does he or she relate on social media sites? How well does the person perform? What can the person do? And can that ability be quantified? Based on the information it finds, Gild comes up with an overall score and helps to predict how well a programmer will perform. Gild's customers can then use that score to compare developers and determine which ones might be the best fit for their organization. The software has become even more useful because companies use it not only to mine for new candidates, but also to assess candidates they are already considering.

Here are some ways technology can be used to enhance operational excellence and help attract and retain top people:

- Aligning the desires of employees with open positions in the organization

- ◆ Vetting candidates and determining the ones with the best fit for the organization

- ◆ Helping to get the message out to the marketplace about organizations and thus raise their profiles

- ◆ Managing the results and accomplishments of employees, as well as their ambitions and desires, essentially having the ability to keep an up-to-date profile on every employee

Managing top people is fast becoming one of the most important keys to operational excellence as increasing numbers of workers pursue flexibility and balance in their work lives. Organizations need to determine how they can best use technology to support this perceived need of employees. Even strategies like remote work and communication technologies will help employees stay connected without having to travel to a physical corporate office every day.

Technology—in particular, its roles in both managing the workforce and enhancing the abilities of workers to do their jobs well wherever they are located—will differentiate the great companies from everyone else. Companies that can remotely harness the power of their people will be much more attractive to up-and-coming stars than those that force them to be in an office every day. Just look at how many people left Yahoo when CEO Marissa Mayer announced that all employees were required to move into a local office and stop working remotely.

> People in the new generation entering the workforce expect a reasonable work-life balance as a basic condition of employment. Organizations need to develop strategies for helping employees have balance and flexibility in their lives. Technology companies like Google, Intel, and Facebook have done a great job with this.

A recent study by Korn/Ferry International revealed that, even though more than two-thirds of organizations know that technology will help them attract and retain top talent, only 26 percent of them are actually doing something about it. Sounds like a great opportunity to leverage technology to help attract and retain the best people.

Innovating and Collaborating

Chapter 4 explained the importance of innovation and how an organization needs not only to encourage innovation, but also to find ways to foster it through collaboration and manage it formally. We looked at the cycle of innovation to see how ideas can be identified, prioritized, and executed successfully. We focused on strategies to increase the level of innovation and how to implement a culture of innovation within your organization. We also looked at how innovation can be accelerated and improved through better collaboration.

We need to remember that generating ideas is great, but organizations must also be able to generate ideas from different places and be able to commercialize those ideas. So we talked about different ways to measure success, which ultimately means the commercialization or use of enhancements and improvements. Let's also remember that innovation can be anything from a small, incremental improvement that enhances an existing product to a disruptive new product or service, one that changes an entire industry.

Indigo Books and Music, the Canadian bookstore chain, is using technology to help gather and prioritize new ideas from customers. Indigo is using technology called SoapBox, which aggregates ideas from customers electronically and then allows customers to vote on their favorite ideas. Indigo puts out its own ideas for new products or improvements to its operations and also allows customers to add their own ideas. Customers are then encouraged to vote on the best ideas, and Indigo has promised to address those ideas that receive the most customer votes. This use of technology not only helps them drive innovation; it also helps increase customer engagement.

With a new strategy that some companies are employing, called "crowd inventing," an organization provides access for people from around the world to innovate collaboratively on a specific invention. Quirky is an organization that supports doing just that. Quirky has created a community of more than 400,000 online members who are would-be inventors. Every week, a group of Quirky employees sifts through the more than 3,000 product idea submissions and narrows them down to the best 15 ideas submitted by members of the community. The group, including some members of the community, then gets together in a room and votes on the 15 ideas (this is called "eval"). If any of the ideas pass a simple majority vote, then Quirky will design, manufacture, and sell the product. Examples of products that Quirky has made include a coin-counting, app-connected piggy bank; a plastic overlay to turn any staircase into a slide; and a device to extract Popsicle-shaped chunks of watermelon.

Once a product is made, Quirky sells it to retail partners at wholesale. Ten cents of every revenue dollar is held as a royalty for those who contributed to the product's creation. The inventor gets 42 percent of royalties; the community that tweaked designs, voted on names, and responded to market research surveys splits the rest. For sales from Quirky's online store, the group divvies up a more generous portion: 30 percent of sales. Quirky, meanwhile, makes a 20–60 percent margin on each item sold to retailers, as well as a $10 fee from those who submit ideas. We may see more of this type of collaboration in the innovation space as it becomes increasingly easy to share ideas with others and to manage those ideas electronically.

Here are some ways that technology can be used to help drive innovation and collaboration:

♦ Electronically gathering ideas for improvement and enhancements

♦ Tracking and monitoring the progress of new ideas

- Providing a forum for gathering feedback on new ideas from around the globe

- Collecting data from diverse sources

- Performing calculations and distilling information that companies are not capable of doing on their own for new inventions

- Allowing people from different parts of the world to collaborate on new ideas and inventions

- Automatically reviewing a large number of ideas and narrowing them down to the best ones based on a common set of criteria

That technology itself needs to be innovative provokes an interesting discussion and makes me ponder the question: How do technology companies use technology to foster innovation? These companies have to be innovative because the needs of their customers are constantly changing and their competitors are constantly coming up with new enhancements and better products and services.

Maybe that is the subject of another book, but it is an interesting question to consider. Often organizations don't follow the same advice they give to their customers. All you technology companies out there! Feel free to send me your thoughts and strategies on how you use technology to stay innovative.

Aligning Strategy and Tactics

Chapter 5 discussed the importance of aligning your strategy with your tactics—how you need to tie your mission to your strategy, your strategy to your execution, and your execution to your operations. That means that everything your organization does should be tied back to the direction in which you want to go and the outcomes you want to achieve. Developing and implementing success metrics that align with that direction is an important component of this effort because those metrics drive employee behavior.

To master the execution of your strategy, you need to have the right mix of priority, accountability, and harmony. This means that you know what is most important for the organization to focus on to achieve its goals (priority), employees take ownership for the success and failure of what they do (accountability), and everything employees do aligns with the direction in which the organization wants to go (harmony). Without all three of these components, your ability to execute will suffer.

How can technology help organizations achieve a more effective alignment of strategy and tactics? Many smaller companies use a project management technology called Basecamp to track projects and activities. With this online software, available for use on computers and also on iPhones, tasks and activities can be tracked from anywhere. Basecamp allows an organization to track multiple initiatives at once, as well as store all relevant documents, and to share those documents and other project details with any user of the system, including customers.

This project management software can help ensure that the activities performed align with the developed strategy. Organizations still need to focus on measuring results and outcomes. Programs like Basecamp do a great job of helping them track activities, and organizations then need to ensure that those activities are helping them move forward toward their strategic objectives. But this software is only a supporting tool for managing that alignment. Leaders still need to ensure that the focus is on outcomes and results, not on the completion of activities.

Here are some ways technology can improve the alignment of strategy and tactics:

- ♦ Tracking the success with metrics put into place to ensure that the activities being performed align with the corporate strategy

- Allowing managers and their employees to be aligned with performance goals and achievements
- Providing communication tools for employees in various locations to meet regularly and ensuring a consistent direction
- Allowing leadership to communicate corporate strategy and expectations using various communication methods

Acquiring and Keeping the Customers You Want

Chapter 6 explained that enhancing customer engagement and retention is about finding ways to bring your customers closer to you—about engaging them in unique ways as you try to increase customer loyalty for your organization. Bringing customers closer and increasing loyalty means that you will create ambassadors for your brand, making the acquisition of new customers faster, cheaper, and easier. Technology can help you accomplish this in many ways.

Starwood Hotels is using technology to enhance the guest experience. Chapter 9 explained how difficult it is for retail organizations to replicate online the experience that customers get when they shop in a physical store and talk to an expert. Some retail chains try to replicate that experience through online reviews and posts by customers. Starwood Hotels is trying that same strategy. Instead of deferring to Web sites like Trip Advisor, where customers can post reviews, Starwood allows hotel guests to post their reviews directly on the Starwood Web site and then directs customers to the Web site to post and read the guest reviews.

The reason this works successfully is that Starwood doesn't filter the reviews, so both positive and negative reviews can be posted. The only filtering that Starwood does is to confirm that the comment came from an actual guest of the hotel before it gets posted. These reviews can also be shared through social media, thus extending the reach even further.

This is an interesting strategy because Starwood doesn't know what guests are going to say. Their comments could be positive or negative, but they force the organization to strive to provide great service and a great experience because it never knows which guests will post their experiences. This strategy also results in a genuine, honest, and transparent perception of the organization. Starwood is taking accountability for how guests are treated and is giving them an open forum to share their views without worrying about reprimand or censure. This strategy also allows Starwood to stay on top of what is being said about them and to drive prospective guests to their Web site. This strategy is likely to result in a lot of goodwill.

The Cleveland Clinic Canada is also using technology effectively to enhance their customer experience, although, in this case, the customers are patients. Cleveland Clinic Canada sees thousands of patients every year for both private care and government-funded procedures, and it keeps detailed electronic records on each one of them. Not only does this mean that when patients arrive at the clinic, all of their medical history is readily available; it also means that this information can be accessed by other medical practitioners. If a patient falls ill in another country, her or his medical history can be accessed and reviewed to ensure that all factors are taken into account. Patients' medical records truly follow them wherever they go, ensuring that they get the best care for their particular needs.

Here are some different ways that technology can be used to enhance customer engagement and retention:

♦ Provide customers with exclusive deals, discounts, events, and information that is available only to them.

♦ Create a forum where customers can share information with each other and the public.

♦ Provide access to valuable insights or information that customers can't get elsewhere.

◆ Keep track of various customers' preferences, likes, and dislikes so that their experience can be customized.

◆ Increase the profile of customers to help them advance their own goals and objectives.

How are you using technology to enhance your customers' experience and improve retention?

Optimizing Speed

Chapter 7 covered the concept of optimizing speed and explored how speed can impact organizational performance. The key concept was that sometimes organizations need to slow down in order to achieve better results. It's important for organizations to implement key indicators that let them know when they need to speed up and when they need to slow down. We looked at some examples of different functions within an organization and the impact that speeding up or slowing down can have. The conclusion was that organizations that manage their speed perform better.

This concept becomes even more interesting when we consider growth and strategy because organizations tend to want to grow more quickly than they should, but they also tend to spend too much time on strategy development. Optimizing speed can help in both areas. Having indicators in place to manage the speed of growth has led to tremendous success for many organizations, and the use of technology has helped achieve those results.

Ensure that rapid growth does not replace sound results and performance. Optimize the speed of growth to take advantage of opportunities while successfully maintaining your existing business.

Amazon is a great example of a company that is using technology to manage growth. Amazon sells almost anything and does it solely online. Amazon also manages the delivery of its products to the end user, and most deliveries are made within a few days.

When Amazon began, it changed the way customers bought products online. To sustain those customers, Amazon had to be able to consistently deliver the right product to the right person and to do it relatively quickly. Amazon invested early not only in online technology but also in state-of-the-art technology for its warehouse and supply chain. The key for Amazon, as they set up technology in both areas, was scalability. The technology needed to be able to handle volumes much larger than what Amazon started with, and the company has done a great job at expanding and simultaneously maintaining operational excellence.

The number of products Amazon sells has gone up dramatically, and its Web site technology has been able to support the additional volume. More important, the supply chain infrastructure has also been able to handle the larger volumes. Amazon outsources the shipping of its products, but it still runs the warehouses responsible for picking and packing those shipments. These warehouses are fully automated with conveyor belts and automated tracking of shipments so that increased growth can be supported.

One of the biggest mistakes organizations make when they grow quickly is to forget that their operations need to stay in line with their new level of sales. Growth doesn't just mean selling more products. It also means expanding the infrastructure to handle the increased volume of products that customers are demanding.

Many organizations focus just on the revenue side. But how can you expect to handle increased volumes if you don't also update your supply chain infrastructure to handle them? Think big, as Amazon did from the outset, and invest in scalable technology that can support dramatically increased volumes.

Here are some ways that technology can help optimize speed:

♦ Providing an automated message when speed indicators get above or below acceptable levels

- Aggregating data around quality, performance, and speed to help determine the optimal speed at which an organization should operate
- Providing an organization the ability to grow exponentially without significant infrastructure changes
- Bringing together geographically disparate members from an organization to collaborate on an initiative

OPERATIONAL EXCELLENCE AND AUTOMATION

One of the most effective ways technology has been used is in automating tasks, whether in a manufacturing facility or in an office environment. Organizations use robots to assemble cars; they use batch processes to compile and aggregate data and the Internet to send out e-mails automatically. It is important to use automation strategically and use it appropriately. The key to using technology for automation is to consider the impact of the process before just automating an activity. As explained earlier in the chapter, when automating a process or activity, we need to ensure that the results will be better and faster, with a minimal amount of effort and maintenance.

When should you consider using technology to automate tasks and activities?

- When you have repetitive tasks that don't require employee intervention or customization
- To aggregate large amounts of data, move it from one system to another, or provide complex analysis of it
- When you use repeatable criteria to assess options and those criteria can be automated to cover multiple areas
- When an activity can be performed more rapidly and more effectively using automation

♦ When the activity is something that employees could not perform on their own

♦ When a low level of resourcing and maintenance is required for that automated activity to be performed effectively

The use of technology to improve operational excellence will become even more prevalent over the coming years. As smartphones become more powerful and as the ability to expand globally becomes easier, the use of technology will increase. Because we never know what the next great technology idea will be, most organizations don't need to stay on top of every new enhancement. They just need to continue to find technology that can improve how they operate daily.

This is the essential question about technology that you need to consider as you evaluate your organization and how it can be improved: How can technology help improve performance and get better results faster?

CHAPTER 11

A BRIGHT FUTURE WITH OPERATIONAL EXCELLENCE

ALTHOUGH THE FUTURE OF YOUR ORGANIZATION will be bright when you relentlessly pursue operational excellence, remember that operational excellence is a journey, not a destination. There is no finish line. There may be many milestones along the way and many points at which an organization can consider its successes, but at no point should it stop pursuing excellence in everything it does.

When you stop pursuing excellence, you let the competition pass you by. We read about organizations every day that have become less relevant because they stopped innovating, stopped growing; they stopped pursuing excellence because they got too comfortable with their success. Research in Motion, Hewlett-Packard, Blockbuster, and even Toyota are just a few examples of companies that reached tremendous levels of success and then forgot to keep moving forward. They forgot to innovate. They made poor strategic decisions. They became complacent. Some were able to bounce back, but others weren't.

There is no finish line. The pursuit of operational excellence is a lifelong journey. And when we continually strive to make improvements in the way we operate, we are able to see improved results all along the way, and that fuels us to continually get better.

Making a commitment to operational excellence really means shifting the way you approach success. Instead of thinking, "I've achieved success, so I can relax now," the best organizations in the world think, "We've achieved success, so what's the next growth opportunity we can take advantage of?" Those organizations are driven to continue succeeding.

THE OPERATIONAL EXCELLENCE CRYSTAL BALL

When I set up my crystal ball to look into the future of operational excellence, I see many changing trends in how organizations approach the way they operate, how they engage with customers, and how they treat employees and other business partners. Figure 2-4 shows my view of the future, the way we will shift from old ways of thinking, to new, more progressive approaches to running organizations.

Instead of focusing on efficiency, organizations need to focus on effectiveness. The difference is that efficiency considers only the volume output for a certain level of resources, whereas effectiveness focuses on doing it right the first time and adding value to the organization.

> The old way of thinking about excellence uses words like *efficiency* and *cost cutting*. The future of operational excellence is described by words like *growth, innovation,* and *effectiveness.*

Instead of focusing on productivity, we need to look at how to get performance boosts. Gone are the days when we measured the outputs of individual employees or departments. We shouldn't care how productive someone is or how long an activity takes; instead, we need to focus on whether an activity helps to achieve a desired outcome or result.

Instead of focusing on cost savings, we need to focus on growth. An organization can't cost-cut its way to success; it can cost-cut its way only to survival. Organizations need to focus on growth in order to avoid complacency. They need to keep driving forward.

Instead of focusing on the elimination of waste, organizations need to focus on driving innovation. Eliminating waste ties into efficiency, but it doesn't push you toward innovation. It helps you improve what you already do, but it doesn't drive you to think about what you could do differently. Innovation drives you in the right direction.

Instead of focusing on standardization, organizations need to focus on customization. Every customer is different and requires a different solution. Organizations need to focus on learning more about their customers and on collaborating with them to provide the best solutions.

Instead of focusing on driving change from the top down, organizations need to focus on engagement and empowerment. This means identifying key internal and external stakeholders and being able to answer the question, "What's in it for them?" Organizations need to articulate a case for change, and getting stakeholders involved early to help shape the change only makes change easier and more successful.

Instead of focusing just on moving faster, organizations need to focus on optimizing speed. In some cases, this will mean moving faster. But in other cases it will mean slowing down. It sounds counterintuitive, but, as Chapter 7 showed, sometimes an organization needs to slow down in order to achieve better results.

Instead of focusing on offering discounted pricing, which only forces customers to think of products as commodities, organizations need to focus on providing value. Their story needs to be about more than just features and benefits and best price. It needs to be about how the products or services can help customers, how they can add value for the customer. In some businesses, price is king, but competing on price won't help most organizations achieve their growth strategy.

Instead of focusing on hiring, organizations need to focus on attracting and recruiting. The difference is that, when you recruit, you are actively targeting specific people for certain roles as opposed to hiring an applicant. And when people are attracted to your organization, the process becomes even easier. Hiring works for roles with repetitive activities or jobs that require a specific skill; for the key management and executive roles, you need to recruit. The other thing to remember is that when a great candidate is attracted to your organization, find a role for that person, even if you need to create a new one.

Instead of focusing on all customers being equal and the mantra that "The customer is always right," focus on customer stratification. Not all customers are created equal, and they shouldn't all be treated equally. Stratify your customers (and your prospects) based on key criteria so that you focus on your best existing customers and your best prospects. Customers should be treated in proportion to the contribution they make to your organization. The key is *to provide a level of service and support that corresponds with the level of purchase the customer is making.* Treat all customers well, but not equally.

Instead of focusing on strategy development, focus on strategy execution. Often organizations take too long in the development of their strategy so that, by the time the strategy is implemented, it is no longer valid. At other times, execution is ineffective because the organization hasn't translated the strategy into operational activities. Ensure that the results, outcomes, and accountabilities that employees are expected to achieve are aligned with the direction in which the organization needs to go.

Finally, instead of focusing on customer satisfaction, focus on customer retention and referrals. The best way to measure whether customers are truly loyal to your brand is if they tell others about you, continue to purchase from you, and are willing to be ambassadors for you. Providing a unique customer experience and actually asking customers for referrals are two great ways to help gauge that loyalty.

Don't wait until the future to make these shifts. Many of the best organizations have already made them, so you need to do it as well. Spend a while staring at Figure 2-4 and identify some changes that you can make in how your organization approaches the various aspects of operational excellence.

YOU'VE ACHIEVED OPERATIONAL EXCELLENCE—NOW WHAT?

Again, operational excellence is not a destination; it is a mind-set that the organization needs to have. It is a collective mentality about abundance and prosperity that sees opportunities to improve around every corner. Instead of worrying about fixing problems, organizations need to focus on where the next opportunity is.

You don't want to just restore the organization to past levels of success; you want to break through to levels of success you never thought possible. Instead of striving for perfection, which will only disappoint you when you don't achieve it, strive for excellence. And that definition of excellence can be whatever you make it.

When you've achieved a certain level of excellence, change your definition of it to ensure that your organization continues to grow and innovate and move forward. Operational excellence is not about benchmarking or comparing your organization to others or to any universal standard of excellence. It's about defining what excellence means for your organization, achieving that excellence, and then developing a new definition of it. Once you achieve that new level of excellence, you redefine it once again. This constant urge to improve ensures that you constantly move forward.

Here are some things the best companies do to ensure they are always striving for new levels of excellence:

♦ They continue to pursue performance improvements by enlisting outside help to keep ideas fresh, by looking for internal successes and how to make them repeatable, and by finding out what is working for others.

♦ They evaluate the performance of their employees and business partners based on the achievement of results and outcomes.

♦ They are not afraid to make tough decisions, even if the decisions go against common practices or old ways of doing business.

♦ They constantly assess the current state of the organization and the stage it is in (growth, expansion, stability, etc.). They then determine what kind of strategy and leadership they need and whether their current strategy and leadership aligns with what they need.

♦ They take pride in being an industry leader and set the bar for other organizations.

Recall the four phases of operational excellence discussed in Chapter 2 and what it takes to achieve mastery. Figure 2-3 serves as a guide to lead you along the path to excellence.

Operational Excellence on the Front Lines

Again, operational excellence is a mind-set that your organization needs to adopt. It is the blood that needs to flow through the veins of your organization. Organizations will be successful when they recognize that operational excellence happens on the front lines. Judgment on those front lines is the heart and soul of operational excellence. It doesn't happen only in the boardroom or in the executive suite. It also needs to happen at the interface where employees deal directly with customers.

Too often, we default to methodologies and tools to avoid having to use judgment, but that approach makes no sense. How can we expect to be successful if we don't trust frontline employees to make the right decisions? The future of operational excellence lies in the empowerment of the organizational front lines to do what's in the best interest of the customer and the organization.

How we measure success will change because we will focus on outcomes and results, not on activities and tasks. How we deal with customers will change because we will focus on growth and retention, not on satisfaction. How we innovate will change because we will focus on where ideas come from and how quickly we can commercialize them, not just on how many ideas we develop. The way we implement strategy will change because the entire organization will develop the strategy; strategy will not be created in a vacuum. How we approach speed will change because we will focus on optimizing speed by using indicators, not on arbitrarily speeding up and slowing down.

The External Impact of Operational Excellence

Throughout this book, we have talked mainly about how operational excellence will impact the results of a single organization. It can increase profitability and performance, employee retention, organizational velocity, and strategic alignment, and it will help you achieve many other great results.

But we have not talked much about the external impact of operational excellence. We haven't talked about how organizations can start to influence the environment around them—customers, suppliers, competitors, even the industry itself. Once organizations begin to achieve excellence, they will look at how to spread that excellence and success to other organizations.

This external impact falls into this final chapter because organizations need to clean up their own backyard before they can help others. My colleague, Dr. Alan Weiss, calls this the oxygen mask principle. On every plane flight you ever take, a flight attendant explains that, in the event of an emergency, you should put on your own oxygen mask before you help others put on theirs. It's the same with operational excellence. You can't effectively work with others to improve overall performance until you have your own mask on.

The fact that an organization has implemented a culture of excellence doesn't mean that they stop pursuing their own performance improvements, but it does mean that they can expand the scope of those improvements. They can look at how they interact with their customers and how they share data and information

Figure 11-1. Expanding Your Sphere of Excellence

with their suppliers. They can look at how they collaborate with other organizations and create joint initiatives that benefit all the organizations involved. They can even look at tackling an industry issue to help raise the bar for everyone in that industry. Figure 11-1 is a schematic of the difference in scope between operational excellence now and where it will go in the future.

With operational excellence, there is no limit on where an impact can be made. The best organizations will continue to expand the scope of excellence and set expectations that their business partners should be pursuing the same level of excellence.

How the Changing World Impacts Operational Excellence

Operational excellence can not only impact things outside an organization, it can be influenced by external factors. The emergence of new economies changes the way organizations make decisions.

We once believed that excellence in manufacturing was sending everything off to China to be produced. We are now seeing the flaws in that theory. As China becomes more successful, their labor costs have risen, and the legal difficulties remain. It is still difficult to ensure a quality product and lead time when managing from the other side of the world. The emergence of countries like Brazil, India, Singapore, South Korea, and some Eastern European countries changes how organizations can approach operational excellence globally.

When you begin to look at the broader spectrum of operational excellence, it can seem more difficult to achieve. The challenges become more complex because they have more moving parts.

But with larger challenges come larger opportunities, and with larger opportunities come larger rewards. The best organizations will create a surrounding sphere of excellence that motivates their organizations, and those organizations they do business with, to constantly pursue ways to improve performance.

The future of operational excellence is now. It doesn't require new technology or a new management methodology. All it requires is an organization dedicated to empowering its people and engaging its customers in a way that promotes collaboration and enhanced performance. Your journey begins now. I hope you have packed the right supplies. You can start by packing this book.

APPENDIX

ARE YOU ON THE PATH TO OPERATIONAL EXCELLENCE?

Figure A-1 is a brief assessment to determine whether you are on a path that leads to operational excellence. Rate yourself on each statement. Are you:

- **Competitive.** You are on par with your competition, and there is not much differentiation.
- **Distinct.** You are above average, ahead of some of the competition, and can clearly differentiate yourself and identify your strengths.
- **Breakthrough.** You are a leader in this area and have very little or no competition.

For a more detailed version of this assessment and the most updated version, please visit http://www.acmconsulting.ca/resources/assessments/operational-excellence-assessment/.

Figure A-1. Are You on the Path to Operational Excellence?

	Competitive	Distinct	Breakthrough
We know when to speed up and when to slow down in order to maximize results.			
We empower our employees (and let them empower themselves) to make decisions that are in the best interests of our customers.			
We only perform activities that align with our strategy.			
We can measure the role that every activity plays in contributing to the achievement of our strategy.			
We know exactly who our customers are and how to communicate with them.			
We stratify our customers to ensure we focus resources effectively.			
We are able to take ideas and effectively turn them into commercial products and services.			
We provide a clear vision on the expected results from our employees and who is accountable for those results.			

INDEX

ABOUT THE AUTHOR

ANDREW MILLER works with world-class organizations to maximize profitability and performance. As a leading expert in operational excellence, he integrates strategies around driving innovation and collaboration; improving customer acquisition, onboarding, and retention; aligning strategy and execution; attracting, hiring, and retaining top people; and optimizing speed.

His clients include the Bank of Nova Scotia, McKesson Canada, 3M Canada, Mount Sinai Hospital, Agnico-Eagle Mines, Women's College Hospital, the Hospital for Sick Children, the Centre for Addiction and Mental Health, and many other world-class institutions.

Andrew has published more than 200 articles, numerous position papers, and three books. His blog, *From Chaos to Order*, is constantly updated with new articles, podcasts, and business insights. He has spoken to corporate and industry audiences across

North America on a variety of topics, and he has been featured in numerous national and international publications.

He has been a visiting professor at the graduate business schools of York University, the University of Victoria, the University of Waterloo, St Mary's University, and various other universities across Canada.

Before starting his firm in 2006, Andrew traveled extensively while holding senior consulting positions with IBM Business Consulting Services and PricewaterhouseCoopers Consulting.

Andrew donates his time to charitable organizations such as Mount Sinai Hospital in Toronto, where he is active in raising money for the hospital and developing the next generation of hospital leadership. Andrew speaks French fluently, is an avid participant in a variety of sports, and is a voracious reader and traveler. He lives in Toronto with his wife, Eryn, and their three children.

Andrew can be reached at andrew@acmconsulting.ca or at (416) 480-1336.